ACCESS TO 200+ SARASOTA RESTAURANT MENUS

The
Little Sarasota
DINING
Book.

2021

UPDATED COVID-19 CARRYOUT & DELIVERY INFO

DINESARASOTA.COM

The Little Sarasota DINING Book.
12th Edition | 2021

To contact us, please send email to:
press@dinesarasota.com

Printed in the USA

10 9 8 7 6 5 4 3 2 1

ISBN 978-0-9862840-6-9

THANK YOU!

Thanks for picking up the 12th edition of our annual Sarasota dining book. This was a tough edition to put together in more ways than are obvious. But, we made it, and you hold the finished product in your hands.

Thanks to Mila Aguiar, Allison Burtoft, Greg Campbell, Ashley Chambers, Robby Clark, Britney Guertin, John Hentschl, Caryn Hodge, Holly Johnson, Laurie Lachowitzer, Russell Matthes, Paul Mattison, Ed Paulsen, Claudia Potes, and Johnny Zaki for contributing to this year's edition. It is great to have such talented people in our community. And, we're grateful for their help.

Jennifer Sistrunk has been turning a local recipe into a work of art for the past five editions. Her illustrated recipes are always creative and imaginative. It's not easy to turn a hot dog into a masterpiece. Thanks!

Lauren Ettinger makes sure that you can read this book without tearing your hair (and eyes) out. Thanks once again for your skillful editing.

As always, thanks to you! Thanks for supporting what we do. We're always striving to make sure that our local Sarasota restaurants get the attention they so richly deserve. It's more important this year than ever before!

A lot has changed since our last edition. I mean, a lot. And, we're wondering the same thing that you are. When will life resume to at least semi-normal? The events of the past months have really brought out the best in our Sarasota restaurant community and the people of Sarasota that support it so well.

Some of our local restaurants haven't been able to overcome the tough odds and circumstances that faced them. While others have survived and even prospered as they faced uncertain market conditions. Staring down the grim realities of a pandemic that threatened their existence, Sarasota restaurant owners resorted to unbelievably creative ways to keep their doors open and continue to serve our local community.

For a time, we even considered not publishing a Sarasota dining book this year. But, in the end, the thought of abandoning our local restaurants at a time when they needed help the most seemed like the wrong thing to do.

This, the 12th annual edition of our dining book is different. This year we are giving you a lot more information on ways you can support your favorite restaurants by using carryout or delivery options that may not have been available in years past. For the first time, each restaurant listing will contain a unique QR code to easily link you to their menu. This will let you make dining decisions quickly and safely.

Things have changed. But, we're hoping the new information contained in this year's Sarasota dining book will help you and our restaurants navigate in a way that is supportive of their efforts to serve our local dining community.

Larry Hoffman
Publisher, dineSarasota.com

2021 DINESARASOTA TOP 50

- ❏ 1   Drunken Poet Cafe
- ❏ 2   Brick's Smoked Meats
- ❏ 3   Siegfried's Restaurant
- ❏ 4   Kiyoshi's Sushi
- ❏ 5   Casey Key Fish House
- ❏ 6   Pier 22
- ❏ 7   Old Salty Dog
- ❏ 8   Munchies 420 Café
- ❏ 9   GROVE Restaurant
- ❏ 10   Turtles on Little Sarasota Bay
- ❏ 11   Pazzo Southside
- ❏ 12   Karl Ehmer's Alpine Steak House
- ❏ 13   Knick's Tavern & Grill
- ❏ 14   Rosemary and Thyme
- ❏ 15   Circo*
- ❏ 16   Island House Tap & Grill
- ❏ 17   Smoqehouse*
- ❏ 18   Yoder's Restaurant
- ❏ 19   1592 Wood Fired Kitchen*
- ❏ 20   Bijou Cafe
- ❏ 21   Grillsmith
- ❏ 22   Mattison's Forty One
- ❏ 23   Duval's Fresh. Local. Seafood.
- ❏ 24   Phillippi Creek Oyster Bar
- ❏ 25   Blasé Southern Style*
- ❏ 26   Cafe Barbosso
- ❏ 27   Ophelia's On The Bay
- ❏ 28   Connors Steak & Seafood
- ❏ 29   Oak & Stone

❏	30	Owen's Fish Camp
❏	31	Café L'Europe
❏	32	A Sprig of Thyme
❏	33	Dry Dock Waterfront Restaurant
❏	34	South Philly Cheesesteaks*
❏	35	The Overton
❏	36	Walt's Fish Market
❏	37	Siesta Key Oyster Bar
❏	38	Sage
❏	39	Speaks Clam Bar
❏	40	Star Thai & Sushi
❏	41	Taste of Asia
❏	42	Marina Jack's
❏	43	Summer House Steak & Seafood
❏	44	Harry's Continental Kitchens
❏	45	The Daiquiri Deck
❏	46	Rosebud's Steakhouse & Seafood
❏	47	Captain Curt's Crab & Oyster Bar
❏	48	Lobster Pot
❏	49	Crab & Fin
❏	50	Jpan Sushi & Grill

HOW TO USE THIS CHECKLIST - Like you really need an explanation for this. But, just in case, here goes. Get out there and eat through our Top 50! We've made it easy for you to keep track of your culinary adventures. These are the restaurants that you've been searching for, clicking on, and downloading on our dineSarasota.com website all year. So, in a way this is really *your* Top 50. And, if you flip to the back of this book, we've left a couple of note pages for you to keep track of your favorites. Go ahead, start your own Sarasota restaurant journal.

* Opened since our last edition.

HOW TO USE THIS BOOK

Thanks for picking up a copy of the latest *Little Sarasota DINING Book*. We're hoping that you're going to use it as your go-to guide to Sarasota dining. Now that you're the proud owner of a copy, we're going to give you some helpful inside tips on how to use the guide.

First off, it's arranged alphabetically. So, if you know the alphabet, you can use our guide. Yes, it's really that easy. It has basic restaurant information in each listing. Name, address, phone… also lists the restaurant's website if you would like to go there for additional information.

In the outlined bar, it will tell you the neighborhood/area that the restaurant is located in, the cuisine it serves, and its relative expense. It's relative to Sarasota, not NYC, keep that in mind.

The hours of operation are also listed. It's nice to know when they are open. We try our best to make this info as accurate as possible. But sometimes, Sarasota restaurants have special seasonal hours. And, with the current COVID situation, things have a tendency to change. If there's a question, it's best to call the restaurant.

For each place we'll also tell you what you can expect. Is it noisy or quiet? Good for kids? Maybe a late night menu. It's not an exhaustive list, just some of the highlights to guide your dining decision making process.

There aren't a lot of mysterious symbols that you have to reference. If you see this *, it means the restaurant has more than one location. We've listed what we consider to be the main one. The other locations are usually listed in the super handy cross reference in the back of the book.

Speaking of the cross reference, here's the scoop. Restaurants are listed in alphabetical order (you're good at that now!). We give you basic info. Name, address, phone. Restaurants are then listed by cuisine type and then by location. So, you can easily find that perfect seafood restaurant on Longboat Key.

QR Codes. These little gems are new for this years edition. If you'll notice, each restaurant listing has a little square box with a bunch of jumbled up dots. That's your easy access to the restaurants menu. Just scan that little code with the QR reader on your smartphone and just like magic, there's the menu! Pretty great, right? Oh, what if I don't have a smartphone? Well, then it might be time for an upgrade! It is 2021 after all.

OK. Here's where things really get interesting. You now know where things are located and what type of food you can expect. But, let's dive in a little deeper. Let's say you're just visiting beautiful, sunny Sarasota AND you've got kids. What would be a good choice? How about celebrating a special occasion or event? Or, maybe you would just like to eat a meal and gaze longingly upon our blue waters. Where's the best spot?

That's where our specialty categories come in. Here are some things to keep in mind. First, we've curated these restaurant lists just for you. Second, these places may not be the only ones in town that fit the description. But, we think they're among the best. Hey, why isn't my favorite pizza place on that list? We're not trying to snub anybody here, but, there's only so much space.

LIVE MUSIC – Really self-explanatory. But, the music ranges from piano bar to acoustic guitar to rock 'n' roll. So, you may want to see who's playing the night you're going. Also, yes, there are other places in town that have live music.

CATERING – You could probably convince most restaurants to cater your twelve person dinner or throw together some to-go food for you to arrange on your own platters. The places listed here do it for REAL. They cater regularly.

EASY ON YOUR WALLET – A little perspective is in order here. Nothing on this list comes close to the McDonald's Dollar Menu (thankfully). That being said, these are some places you could go and not dip into your kids 529 plan to pay the bill. Something to keep in mind, "Easy on the wallet" depends a little on how big your billfold is. These restaurants won't break the budget.

NEW – No explanation necessary. These restaurants are "relatively" new. Some have been open longer than others. But, they've opened since our last edition.

SPORTS + FOOD + FUN – If the big game is on and you want to see it. Here are some places that do that well. Lots of places have a TV in the bar. These go above and beyond that.

GREAT BURGERS – Nothing evokes a more passionate outcry of food worship than a good burger debate. The truth is, we don't want to do that. But, this will probably start a conversation at a minimum. Again, lots of spots serve burgers. In our opinion, these standout.

NICE WINE LIST – Hmmm… A 2006 Cabernet or a 2015 Pouilly-Fuissé? That is one tough question. No "wine in a box" here. These restaurants all have a sturdy wine list and are proud of it. If you can be a little intimidated with the task of choosing a wine, relax. These spots usually have someone to hold your hand and walk you through it.

A BEAUTIFUL WATER VIEW – Nothing says Florida like a picture perfect view of the water. And, these places have that. The food runs the gamut from bar food to fine dining.

LATER NIGHT MENU – This is not New York, it is not Miami or Chicago either. That is the context with which you should navigate this list. Notice we said "LATER" night menu and NOT "late night menu." We're a reasonably early dining town. The places listed here are open past the time when half of Sarasota is safely tucked in bed. They all might not be 1AM, but, we do have a 4:20AMer in there!

SARASOTA FINE DINING – It's not great when people look down their nose at our upscale dining scene. We have some damn good chefs here in Sarasota. And, they're showing off their skills every single day. They should be celebrated. This list may not contain Le Bernardin, Alinea, or The French Laundry. But, we have some REAL contenders.

Lastly, there is always the question, "How do these restaurants get into this book?" They are selected based on their yearly popularity on dineSarasota.com. These are the restaurants that YOU are interested in. You've been searching for them on our website all year long. There are no advertisements here. So, that being said, you can't buy your way in. It's all you. This is really YOUR guide. And, I must say you have great taste!

A SPRIG OF THYME
1962 Hillview Street
941-330-8890
www.asprigofthymesrq.com

SOUTHSIDE VILLAGE	EUROPEAN	COST: $$

HOURS: Tues-Sat, 5PM to 9PM
CLOSED SUNDAY & MONDAY (SUMMER ONLY)

WHAT TO EXPECT: Upscale, casual • Good for a date
European bistro feel • Good wine list

CARRYOUT/DELIVERY INFO: Full menu available for carryout.
Curbside and contactless pick up. Delivery not available.

SOME BASICS

SCAN FOR MENU

Reservations:	YES
Spirits:	BEER/WINE
Parking:	STREET
Outdoor Dining:	YES

ANDREA'S
2085 Siesta Drive
941-951-9200
andreasrestaurantsrq.com

SOUTHGATE	ITALIAN	COST: $$$

HOURS: Mon-Sat, 5PM to 10PM
CLOSED SUNDAY (summer only)

WHAT TO EXPECT: Nice wine list • Quiet restaurant atmosphere
Upscale Italian cuisine • Great special occasion place

CARRYOUT/DELIVERY INFO: Special menu for carryout and
delivery. Contactless & curbside pick up available. Phone-in only.
Delivery not available. Cash or check for delivery.

SOME BASICS

SCAN FOR MENU

Reservations:	YES
Spirits:	BEER/WINE
Parking:	LOT
Outdoor Dining:	NO

ANNA MARIA OYSTER BAR

6906 14th Street W.*
941-758-7880
oysterbar.net

BRADENTON	SEAFOOD	COST: $$

HOURS: Sun-Thur, 11AM to 9PM • Fri-Sat, 11AM to 10PM

WHAT TO EXPECT: Good for kids • Casual, family atmosphere
Large menu • FLRA COVID-19 Seal of Commitment

CARRYOUT/DELIVERY INFO: Full menu carryout available.
Phone-in ordering. Curbside pick up. Special menu for delivery.
Service through Uber Eats, Grubhub and DoorDash.

SCAN FOR MENU

SOME BASICS

Reservations:	8 OR MORE
Spirits:	FULL BAR
Parking:	LOT
Outdoor Dining:	YES

ANTHONY'S ITALIAN DELI & EATERY　　NEW

4944 South Tamiami Trail (The Landings)
941-365-2998
anthonys-deli.com

SOUTH TRAIL	DELI	COST: $$

HOURS: Daily, Lunch & Dinner

WHAT TO EXPECT: Deli sandwiches • Good for a carryout
Landing's location = lots of parking • Catering available

CARRYOUT/DELIVERY INFO: Full menu plus specials available for
carryout. Curbside pick up. Delivery not available.

SCAN FOR MENU

SOME BASICS

Reservations:	NO
Spirits:	BEER/WINE
Parking:	LOT
Outdoor Dining:	NO

ANTOINE'S RESTAURANT
1100 North Tuttle Avenue
941-331-1400
antoinessarasota.com

GRAND SLAM PLAZA	EUROPEAN	COST: $$$

HOURS: Mon, 5PM to 9PM • Fri-Sun, 5PM to 9PM
CLOSED TUESDAY, WEDNESDAY & THURSDAY

WHAT TO EXPECT: Nice wine list • Intimate dining
Online reservations • Lots of parking

CARRYOUT/DELIVERY INFO: Full menu available for carryout
Friday to Sunday. Special carryout menu Monday. Delivery
available thorough DoorDash.

SOME BASICS
Reservations:	YES
Spirits:	BEER/WINE
Parking:	LOT
Outdoor Dining:	NO

SCAN FOR MENU

APOLLONIA GRILL
8235 Cooper Creek Boulevard*
941-359-4816
apolloniagrill.com

UPARK	GREEK	COST: $$

HOURS: Mon-Thur, 11:30AM to 9PM • Fri & Sat, 11:30AM to 10PM
Sunday, 11:30AM to 8:30PM

WHAT TO EXPECT: Good for groups • Family owned
Casual dining • Lots of parking • Also a Landings location

CARRYOUT/DELIVERY INFO: Most menu items available for
carryout and delivery. Curbside and contactless pick up.
Delivery available through DoorDash.

SOME BASICS
Reservations:	YES
Spirits:	FULL BAR
Parking:	LOT
Outdoor Dining:	YES

SCAN FOR MENU

BAKER AND WIFE

2157 Siesta Drive
941-960-1765
bakerwife.com

SOUTHGATE	AMERICAN	COST: $$

HOURS: Thur-Sat, 5PM to 9PM

WHAT TO EXPECT: Artisan pizza • Casual atmosphere
Lots of dessert choices • OpenTable Reservations

CARRYOUT/DELIVERY INFO: Online ordering available. Full menu available for carryout. Delivery not available.

SCAN FOR MENU

SOME BASICS

Reservations:	YES
Spirits:	FULL BAR
Parking:	LOT
Outdoor Dining:	YES

BAVARO'S PIZZA NAPOLETANA & PASTERIA

27 Fletcher Avenue
941-552-9131
bavarospizza.com

DOWNTOWN	PIZZA	COST: $$

HOURS: Sun-Thur, 5PM to 9PM • Fri & Sat, 5PM to 10PM

WHAT TO EXPECT: Casual Italian • Good for families • Pizza!
Gluten free options • OpenTable reservations

CARRYOUT/DELIVERY INFO: Order online or through Toast app. Full menu available for carryout and delivery. Delivery available through Uber Eats and Bite Squad.

SCAN FOR MENU

SOME BASICS

Reservations:	YES
Spirits:	FULL BAR
Parking:	LOT/STREET
Outdoor Dining:	YES

BEACH BISTRO

6600 Gulf Drive
941-778-6444
beachbistro.com

HOLMES BEACH	AMERICAN	COST: $$$$

HOURS: Daily, 5PM to 10PM

WHAT TO EXPECT: Fine dining • Beautiful gulf views • Romantic
Newly upgraded HVAC for a safe dining experience

CARRYOUT/DELIVERY INFO: Carryout and delivery not available.

SCAN FOR MENU

SOME BASICS

Reservations:	YES
Spirits:	FULL BAR
Parking:	VALET
Outdoor Dining:	YES

THE BEACH HOUSE RESTAURANT

200 Gulf Drive North
941-779-2222
beachhousedining.com

BRADENTON BEACH	AMERICAN	COST: $$$

HOURS: Daily, 11:30AM to 10PM

WHAT TO EXPECT: Great for a date • Florida seafood
Nice wine list • Lots of outdoor dining space

CARRYOUT/DELIVERY INFO: Order online or through Toast app.
Full menu is available for carryout. Delivery not available.

SCAN FOR MENU

SOME BASICS

Reservations:	NO
Spirits:	FULL BAR
Parking:	LOT
Outdoor Dining:	YES

BEVARDI'S SALUTE! RESTAURANT

23 North Lemon Avenue
941-365-1020
salutesarasota.com

DOWNTOWN	ITALIAN	COST: $$

HOURS: Tue-Thur, 4PM to 10PM • Fri & Sat, 4PM to 11PM
Sun, 4PM to 10PM • CLOSED MONDAY

WHAT TO EXPECT: Live music • In-house catering
OpenTable reservations • Nice outdoor dining

CARRYOUT/DELIVERY INFO: Online ordering. Full menu available
for carryout and delivery. Delivery available through Bite Squad.

SCAN FOR MENU

SOME BASICS
Reservations:	YES
Spirits:	FULL BAR
Parking:	STREET/LOT
Outdoor Dining:	YES

BIG WATER FISH MARKET

6641 Midnight Pass Road
941-554-8101
bigwaterfishmarket.com

SIESTA KEY	SEAFOOD	COST: $$

HOURS: Mon-Sat, 11AM to 9PM • Sunday, 12PM to 8PM

WHAT TO EXPECT: Fresh fish market • Casual dining
SK south bridge location • Key lime pie!

CARRYOUT/DELIVERY INFO: Online menu. Phone-in ordering
only. Curbside pick up available. Delivery not available.

SCAN FOR MENU

SOME BASICS
Reservations:	NO
Spirits:	BEER/WINE
Parking:	LOT
Outdoor Dining:	NO

BIJOU CAFÉ

1287 First Street
941-366-8111
bijoucafe.net

DOWNTOWN	AMERICAN	COST: $$$

HOURS: Mon-Fri, 11:30AM to 2PM • Mon-Sat, 5PM to Close
CLOSED SUNDAY (summer only)

WHAT TO EXPECT: Great for a date • Excellent wine list
OpenTable reservations • Private dining program

CARRYOUT/DELIVERY INFO: Online ordering available. Full menu available for carryout. Curbside and contactless pick up. Delivery not available.

SOME BASICS

SCAN FOR MENU

Reservations:	YES
Spirits:	FULL BAR
Parking:	VALET
Outdoor Dining:	YES

BLASÉ SOUTHERN STYLE   NEW

1920 Hillview Street
941-312-6850
blasebistro.com

SOUTHSIDE VILLAGE	AMERICAN	COST: $$$

HOURS: Mon-Fri, 11:30AM to 2PM • Mon-Sat, 5PM to Close
CLOSED SUNDAY (summer only)

WHAT TO EXPECT: Great for a date • Live music
OpenTable reservations • Good For private events

CARRYOUT/DELIVERY INFO: Online ordering available. Full menu available for carryout and delivery. Curbside pick up. Delivery available through Bite Squad.

SOME BASICS

SCAN FOR INFO

Reservations:	YES
Spirits:	FULL BAR
Parking:	VALET
Outdoor Dining:	YES

BLU KOUZINA

25 North Boulevard of Presidents
941-388-2619
blukouzina.com/US

ST. ARMANDS	GREEK	COST: $$$

HOURS: Mon-Fri, 8:30AM to 3PM • Sat & Sun, 8AM to 3PM
Mon-Sun, 5PM to 9:30PM

WHAT TO EXPECT: Nice wine list • REAL Greek cuisine
OpenTable reservations • Many small plate appetizers

CARRYOUT/DELIVERY INFO: Full menu is available for carryout.
Curbside pick up available. Delivery not available.

SCAN FOR MENU

SOME BASICS

Reservations:	YES
Spirits:	BEER/WINE
Parking:	STREET
Outdoor Dining:	YES

BOCA SARASOTA

19 South Lemon Avenue
941-256-3565
bocasarasota.com

DOWNTOWN	AMERICAN	COST: $$

HOURS: Mon-Fri, 11AM to 10PM • Sat, 10AM to 11PM
Sun, 10AM to 10PM

WHAT TO EXPECT: Sat & Sun Brunch • Online reservations
Classic cocktails • Craft beer selections

CARRYOUT/DELIVERY INFO: Online ordering. Full menu available
for carryout and delivery. Curbside pick up. Delivery available
through Uber Eats.

SCAN FOR MENU

SOME BASICS

Reservations:	YES
Spirits:	FULL BAR
Parking:	STREET
Outdoor Dining:	YES

THE BODHI TREE

1938 Adams Lane
941-702-8552
bodhitreecafesrq.com

TOWLES COURT	MEDITERRANEAN	COST: $$

HOURS: Thur-Sat, 5PM to 8:30PM

WHAT TO EXPECT: Causal atmosphere • Daily specials
Family owned and operated

CARRYOUT/DELIVERY INFO: Special menu available for carryout
and delivery. Curbside pick up. Free delivery in the downtown
Sarasota area.

SCAN FOR MENU

SOME BASICS

Reservations:	YES
Spirits:	BEER/WINE
Parking:	LOT/STREET
Outdoor Dining:	YES

BONJOUR FRENCH CAFÉ

5214 Ocean Boulevard
941-346-0600
bonjourfrenchcafe.com

SIESTA KEY	FRENCH	COST: $$

HOURS: Daily, 7AM to 2:30PM

WHAT TO EXPECT: Super casual • Great outdoor dining
Great crepes!

CARRYOUT/DELIVERY INFO: Full menu available for carryout.
Delivery not available.

SCAN FOR MENU

SOME BASICS

Reservations:	NONE
Spirits:	BEER/WINE
Parking:	STREET
Outdoor Dining:	YES

BRICK'S SMOKED MEATS

1528 State Street
941-993-1435
brickssmokedmeats.com

DOWNTOWN	BBQ	COST: $$

HOURS: Sun-Thur, 11AM to 10PM • Fri & Sat, 11AM to 11PM

WHAT TO EXPECT: State Street garage • BBQ, BBQ, BBQ
Good local beer list • Upbeat atmosphere • Catering

CARRYOUT/DELIVERY INFO: Online Ordering. Full menu available
for carryout and delivery. Curbside pick up. Delivery available
through Bite Squad, Uber Eats and DoorDash.

SCAN FOR MENU

SOME BASICS

Reservations:	YELP WAITLIST
Spirits:	FULL BAR
Parking:	STREET/GARAGE
Outdoor Dining:	YES

BRIDGE STREET BISTRO

111 Gulf Drive South
941-782-1122
bridgestreetbistroonline.com

BRADENTON BEACH	AMERICAN	COST: $$

HOURS: Sun-Thur, 5PM to 9PM • Fri & Sat, 5PM to 10PM

WHAT TO EXPECT: Florida feel • Great for a date
Casual but upscale • Water view

CARRYOUT/DELIVERY INFO: Special menu for carryout.
Phone-in carryout only (no online ordering). Contactless pick up
available. Delivery not available.

SCAN FOR MENU

SOME BASICS

Reservations:	YES
Spirits:	FULL BAR
Parking:	LOT
Outdoor Dining:	YES

BRIDGES RESTAURANT

202 North Tamiami Trail (Embassy Suites Sarasota)
941-536-9107
bridgessarasota.com

DOWNTOWN	AMERICAN	COST: $$$

HOURS: Mon-Sat, 12PM to 8PM
CLOSED SUNDAY

WHAT TO EXPECT: Upscale dining experience • Water view
Daily specials • 15% discount to first responders

CARRYOUT/DELIVERY INFO: Full menu is available for carryout.
Also, special deli items (call for availability). Delivery not available.

SOME BASICS

SCAN FOR MENU

Reservations:	YES
Spirits:	FULL BAR
Parking:	VALET
Outdoor Dining:	NO

BRINE SEAFOOD & RAW BAR

NEW

2250 Gulf Gate Drive
941-404-5639
BrineSarasota.com

GULF GATE	SEAFOOD	COST: $$

HOURS: Lunch and dinner daily

WHAT TO EXPECT: Raw bar • Northeastern style seafood
Real Maryland style lump meat crab cakes

CARRYOUT/DELIVERY INFO: Full menu available for carryout.
Delivery not available.

SOME BASICS

SCAN FOR MENU

Reservations:	NO
Spirits:	FULL BAR
Parking:	LOT/STREET
Outdoor Dining:	NO

What Is Savor Sarasota Restaurant Week?

Savor Sarasota Restaurant Week is an annual two-week celebration of our award-winning culinary community beloved by locals and visitors alike. From June 1-14, dozens of restaurants offer special multi-course, prix-fixe lunch and dinner menus for $16 and $32 featuring unique entrees, appetizers, desserts, cocktails and any other signature items the destination may be cooking up!

Savor Sarasota began in 2006 as an effort to help independent restaurants thrive in the summer, formerly an "offseason" for dining in the destination. From 25 eateries in the first year to nearly 100 in 2019, Savor has grown from humble beginnings to something highly anticipated by both businesses and customers looking to try new places they might otherwise overlook.

During Savor Sarasota, Visit Sarasota County (VSC) executes a multi-level marketing campaign for the promotion of participating restaurants across digital, print and social media platforms along with robust public relations efforts with media and influencers. Beyond Savor, VSC continues many of these marketing efforts to position Sarasota County as a culinary destination along Florida's Gulf Coast®.

Savor Sarasota is about experiencing your favorite restaurants and trying new ones in an upscale yet charming beach destination. When you start your summer in Sarasota County, you can count on warm weather, relaxation, and a full stomach!

Visit Sarasota County (VSC) leads and supports the tourism industry in Sarasota County by providing the highest quality, and most innovative, marketing programs and promotions to ensure the continued growth of tourism and travel from visitors around the world. To learn more, visit www.visitsarasota.com.

BURNS COURT BISTRO
401 South Pineapple Avenue
941-312-6633
theburnscourtcafe.com

BURNS COURT	AMERICAN	COST: $$

HOURS: Mon-Sat, 9:30AM to 4PM • Brunch Sat, 9:30AM to 2PM
CLOSED SUNDAY

WHAT TO EXPECT: Small and cozy atmosphere
Good wine list • Great pastries

CARRYOUT/DELIVERY INFO: Full menu available for carryout and delivery. Curbside pick up. Delivery through Bite Squad and Uber Eats.

SCAN FOR MENU

SOME BASICS
Reservations:	NO
Spirits:	BEER/WINE
Parking:	STREET
Outdoor Dining:	YES

BUSHIDO IZAYAKI
3688 Webber Street
941-217-5635
bushidosushisrq.com

	SUSHI	COST: $$

HOURS: Mon-Sat, 3PM to 9:30PM
CLOSED SUNDAY

WHAT TO EXPECT: Casual sushi • Good for families
Good sake selection

CARRYOUT/DELIVERY INFO: Full menu available for carryout. Curbside and contactless pick up. Delivery not available.

SCAN FOR MENU

SOME BASICS
Reservations:	YES
Spirits:	BEER/WINE
Parking:	LOT
Outdoor Dining:	NO

CAFÉ BACI

4001 South Tamiami Trail
941-921-4848
www.cafebacisarasota.com

SOUTH TRAIL	ITALIAN	COST: $$

HOURS: Tues-Sun, 4PM to 9:30PM
CLOSED MONDAY

WHAT TO EXPECT: Family owned since '91 • Private room available
Older dining crowd

CARRYOUT/DELIVERY INFO: Full menu available for carryout.
Curbside and contactless pick up. Delivery available through Bite
Squad.

SCAN FOR MENU

SOME BASICS

Reservations:	YES
Spirits:	FULL BAR
Parking:	LOT
Outdoor Dining:	NO

CAFÉ BARBOSSO

5501 Palmer Crossing Circle
941-922-7999
cafebarbosso.com

PALMER CROSSING	ITALIAN	COST: $$

HOURS: Tues-Sun, 4PM to 9PM • CLOSED MONDAY

WHAT TO EXPECT: Authentic NYC Italian • Casual dining
Fun dining experience • Good for groups

CARRYOUT/DELIVERY INFO: Full menu available for carryout
including family meals. Contactless, curbside pick up. Delivery
not available.

SCAN FOR MENU

SOME BASICS

Reservations:	YES
Spirits:	FULL BAR
Parking:	LOT
Outdoor Dining:	YES

CAFÉ EPICURE

1298 North Palm Avenue
941-366-5648
www.cafeepicure.com

DOWNTOWN	ITALIAN	COST: $$

HOURS: Daily, 11:45AM to 10:30PM

WHAT TO EXPECT: Great for a date • Wood fired pizza
Casual Italian fare • Palm garage

CARRYOUT/DELIVERY INFO: Full menu available for carryout and delivery. No curbside service. Delivery through Bite Squad, Uber Eats and Grubhub.

SOME BASICS

SCAN FOR MENU

Reservations:	YES
Spirits:	FULL BAR
Parking:	STREET/PALM GARAGE
Outdoor Dining:	YES

CAFÉ GABBIANO

5104 Ocean Boulevard
941-349-1423
cafegabbiano.com

SIESTA KEY	ITALIAN	COST: $$$

HOURS: Daily, 5PM to 10PM

WHAT TO EXPECT: Great wine list • Siesta Village location
Lots of parking • OpenTable reservations

CARRYOUT/DELIVERY INFO: Online ordering available. Full menu available for carryout and delivery. Curbside and contactless pick up. Delivery through Bite Squad and DoorDash.

SOME BASICS

SCAN FOR MENU

Reservations:	YES
Spirits:	FULL BAR
Parking:	LOT
Outdoor Dining:	YES

CAFÉ IN THE PARK

2010 Adams Lane (Payne Park)
941-361-3032
www.cafeinthepark.org

DOWNTOWN	DELI	COST: $

HOURS: Sat-Thur, 11AM to 6PM • Fri, 11AM to 9:30PM

WHAT TO EXPECT: Super casual • Good for families & kids
Live music Fridays • Great outdoor dining

CARRYOUT/DELIVERY INFO: Most menu items available for
carryout and delivery. Also, daily specials. Curbside pick up.
Delivery through Bite Squad and Uber Eats.

SCAN FOR MENU

SOME BASICS

Reservations:	NO
Spirits:	NONE
Parking:	LOT
Outdoor Dining:	YES

CAFÉ L'EUROPE

431 St. Armands Circle
941-388-4415
cafeleurope.net

ST. ARMANDS	EUROPEAN	COST: $$$

HOURS: Tues-Fri, 4PM to 9PM • Sat, 11:30AM to 9PM
Sun, 11:30AM to 4PM • CLOSED MONDAY

WHAT TO EXPECT: Great wine list • Catering available
Outdoor cafe style dining • OpenTable reservations

CARRYOUT/DELIVERY INFO: Full menu available for carryout.
Curbside and contactless pick up. Delivery not available.

SCAN FOR MENU

SOME BASICS

Reservations:	YES
Spirits:	FULL BAR
Parking:	VALET/STREET
Outdoor Dining:	YES

CAFÉ LONGET

239 Miami Avenue W
941-244-2643
cafelonget.com

VENICE	FRENCH	COST: $$$

HOURS: Lunch: Mon-Fri, 12:00PM to 2:30PM
Dinner: Mon-Sat, 5:00PM to 9PM • CLOSED SUNDAY

WHAT TO EXPECT: Traditional French fare • Relaxed atmosphere
Homemade bread • OpenTable reservations

CARRYOUT/DELIVERY INFO: Most menu items available for
carryout. Delivery not available.

SOME BASICS

SCAN FOR MENU

Reservations:	YES
Spirits:	BEER/WINE
Parking:	STREET
Outdoor Dining:	YES

CAFÉ VENICE

101 West Venice Avenue
941-484-1855
cafevenicerestaurantandbar.com

VENICE	AMERICAN	COST: $$

HOURS: Tue-Sat, 11:30AM to 9PM
CLOSED SUNDAY & MONDAY

WHAT TO EXPECT: Casual dining • Live music • Downtown Venice
Catering available • Good for groups

CARRYOUT/DELIVERY INFO: Full menu available for carryout.
Curbside and contactless pick up. Delivery not available.

SOME BASICS

SCAN FOR MENU

Reservations:	YES
Spirits:	BEER/WINE
Parking:	STREET
Outdoor Dining:	YES

CAPTAIN BRIAN'S SEAFOOD RESTAURANT

8421 North Tamiami Trail
941-351-4492
captainbrianssseafood.com

NORTH TRAIL	SEAFOOD	COST: $$

HOURS: Mon-Sat, 11AM to 8PM
CLOSED SUNDAY

WHAT TO EXPECT: Casual dining • Older dining crowd
Good for groups • Locally owned 30+ years

CARRYOUT/DELIVERY INFO: Most menu items available for
carryout and delivery. Curbside pick up. Delivery through
Uber Eats.

SCAN FOR MENU

SOME BASICS

Reservations:	YES
Spirits:	FULL BAR
Parking:	STREET/VALET
Outdoor Dining:	YES

CAPTAIN CURT'S CRAB & OYSTER BAR

1200 Old Stickney Point Road
941-349-3885
captaincurts.com

SIESTA KEY	SEAFOOD	COST: $$

HOURS: Daily, 11AM to 2AM

WHAT TO EXPECT: Good for kids • Super casual • Lots of seafood
Ohio State football HQ • Live music

CARRYOUT/DELIVERY INFO: Online Ordering available. Full
menu available for carryout. Walk-up carryout station for pick up.
Delivery not available.

SCAN FOR MENU

SOME BASICS

Reservations:	NO
Spirits:	FULL BAR
Parking:	LOT
Outdoor Dining:	YES

CARAGIULOS

69 South Palm Avenue
941-951-0866
caragiulos.com

DOWNTOWN	ITALIAN	COST: $$

HOURS: Daily, 4PM to 9PM

WHAT TO EXPECT: Casual dining • Palm Ave. gallery district
Good for kids • Good for groups

CARRYOUT/DELIVERY INFO: Online ordering available (special menu). Curbside pick up. Delivery available through Grubhub and DoorDash.

SOME BASICS

SCAN FOR MENU

Reservations:	YES
Spirits:	FULL BAR
Parking:	STREET/VALET
Outdoor Dining:	YES

CASEY KEY FISH HOUSE

801 Blackburn Point Road
941-966-1901
caseykeyfishhouse.com

OSPREY	SEAFOOD	COST: $$

HOURS: Daily, 11:30AM to 9PM

WHAT TO EXPECT: Vacation atmosphere • Local seafood
Boat docks • Old Florida feel • Live music

CARRYOUT/DELIVERY INFO: Full menu is available for carryout. Curbside pick up during non-peak hours. Delivery not avaialble.

SOME BASICS

SCAN FOR MENU

Reservations:	NO
Spirits:	FULL BAR
Parking:	LOT
Outdoor Dining:	YES

CASSARIANO ITALIAN EATERY

313 W. Venice Avenue*
941-786-1000
cassariano.com

VENICE	ITALIAN	COST: $$$

HOURS: Lunch, Mon-Sat, 11AM to 3PM
Dinner, Mon-Sat 4:30 to Close • Sunday, 5PM to Close

WHAT TO EXPECT: Nice wine list • A UTC location, too
Great desserts • OpenTable reservations

CARRYOUT/DELIVERY INFO: Online ordering for delivery only.
Curbside pick up available for phone in carryout. Delivery through
Uber Eats and DoorDash.

SCAN FOR MENU

SOME BASICS

Reservations:	YES
Spirits:	FULL BAR
Parking:	LOT
Outdoor Dining:	YES

C'EST LA VIE!

1553 Main Street
941-906-9575
cestlaviesarasota.com

DOWNTOWN	FRENCH	COST: $$

HOURS: Mon-Wed, 7:30AM to 6PM • Thur-Sat, 7:30AM to 10PM
Sunday Brunch, 8:30AM to 4:30PM

WHAT TO EXPECT: Outdoor tables • Relaxed cafe dining
Fantastic bakery • OpenTable reservations

CARRYOUT/DELIVERY INFO: Online ordering available for
carryout (both locations). Delivery available through DoorDash.

SCAN FOR MENU

SOME BASICS

Reservations:	YES
Spirits:	BEER/WINE
Parking:	STREET
Outdoor Dining:	YES

CHA CHA COCONUTS TROPICAL BAR
417 St. Armands Circle
941-388-3300
chacha-coconuts.com

ST. ARMANDS	AMERICAN	COST: $$

HOURS: Sun-Thur, 11AM to 9PM • Fri & Sat, 11AM to 11PM

WHAT TO EXPECT: Good for kids • Lot of outdoor tables
Bustling atmosphere

CARRYOUT/DELIVERY INFO: Full menu available for carryout.
Curbside and contactless pick up, Delivery is not available.

SCAN FOR MENU

SOME BASICS
Reservations:	NO
Spirits:	FULL BAR
Parking:	STREET/GARAGE/VALET
Outdoor Dining:	YES

CHIANTI RISTORANTE ITALIANO
3900 Clark Road
941-952-3186
chiantisarasota.com

	ITALIAN	COST: $$

HOURS: Daily, 4PM to 8PM

WHAT TO EXPECT: Casual atmosphere • Classic Italian cuisine
Happy Hour

CARRYOUT/DELIVERY INFO: Full menu available for carryout and
delivery. Curbside pick up. Delivery available through DoorDash,
Grub Hub and Uber Eats.

SCAN FOR MENU

SOME BASICS
Reservations:	YES
Spirits:	FULL BAR
Parking:	LOT
Outdoor Dining:	YES

dineSarasota
Essentials

Florida Restaurant and Lodging Association Seal of Commitment

By Allison Burtoft, FL Restaurant & Lodging Assn.

Across Florida, restaurants and hotels are going above and beyond to heighten safety and sanitation standards by achieving the Florida Restaurant and Lodging Association (FRLA) Seal of Commitment. On July 1st, FRLA launched the Seal of Commitment: FRLA's highest designation for hospitality safety and sanitation standards. It is a promise to guests that an establishment is committed to keeping their space clean and safe and that their staff is well trained. In a post COVID-19 environment, cleanliness is a vital factor for guest comfort. When guests see a Seal of Commitment on an establishment's door, they can feel confident that it will be clean and safe.

When businesses began to reopen following the COVID-19 pandemic, many restaurants saw a need to improve guest confidence to return to dining rooms. During these unprecedented times, the FRLA Seal of Commitment was the perfect opportunity for these establishments to provide more training to their staff, enhance their cleaning, and adjust their Standard Operating Procedures.

Seal of Commitment designees are required to go above and beyond what is required for safety and sanitation training. To qualify for the Seal of Commitment, the establishment must complete current food manager, all food safety, and an FRLA COVID-19 Sanitation and Safety Course. Once all the courses are complete, and qualifications are met, an FRLA staff member visits the establishment to confirm all requirements have been met and award the Seal.

The greater Sarasota area has led the way for Seal of Commitment designees. The first restaurant to achieve the Seal of Commitment was Anna Maria Oyster Bar in Ellenton, FL. "We wanted to be the first restaurant to receive the FRLA Seal of Commitment as we feel it is so important to not only talk the talk but walk the walk in keeping our restaurants safe and secure for our guests and our staff during these crazy times," said John Horne, Owner and President, Anna Maria Oyster Bar. "Having the FRLA's Seal behind us lets our guests know loud and clear that we are committed to everyone's healthy return to our and all restaurants in Florida." Since the launch, many other Sarasota area establishments have also achieved the Seal of Commitment.

The Seal of Commitment program is available to all hospitality establishments in Florida – including FRLA members and non-members. For more information about the FRLA Seal of Commitment, including a full list of designees across the state, please visit https://frla.org/sealofcommitment. Look for this seal on restaurant listings in this guide.

CIRCO

1435 2nd Street
941-253-0978
www.circosrq.com

DOWNTOWN	MEXICAN	COST: $$

HOURS: Mon-Thur, 11AM to 10PM • Fri, 12PM to 11PM
Sat, 11AM to 11PM • Sun, 11AM to 8PM

WHAT TO EXPECT: Super casual • "Taco & Bourbon Joint"
Good for a group • Catering available

CARRYOUT/DELIVERY INFO: Online ordering. Curbside and contactless pick up available on request. Delivery is available through Bite Squad, Uber Eats and DoorDash.

SOME BASICS
Reservations:	NO
Spirits:	FULL BAR
Parking:	STREET/GARAGE
Outdoor Dining:	YES

SCAN FOR MENU

CLASICO ITALIAN CHOPHOUSE

1341 Main Street
941-957-0700
clasicosrq.com

DOWNTOWN	ITALIAN	COST: $$

HOURS: Mon & Tue, 11AM to 11PM • Wed-Fri, 11AM to 12AM
Sat, 10AM to 12AM • Sun, 10AM to 11AM

WHAT TO EXPECT: Great for a date • Live music • Energetic scene
Sat. & Sun. brunch

CARRYOUT/DELIVERY INFO: Online ordering. Full menu available
for carryout and delivery. Curbside pick up. Delivery available
through Uber Eats, Grubhub and DoorDash.

SCAN FOR MENU

SOME BASICS

Reservations:	YES
Spirits:	FULL BAR
Parking:	STREET/PALM GARAGE
Outdoor Dining:	YES

THE COLUMBIA RESTAURANT

411 St. Armands Circle
941-388-3987
columbiarestaurant.com

ST. ARMANDS	CUBAN/SPANISH	COST: $$

HOURS: Sun-Thur, 11AM to 9PM • Fri & Sat, 11AM to 10PM

WHAT TO EXPECT: Fantastic sangria • Excellent service
OpenTable reservations • Very busy in season

CARRYOUT/DELIVERY INFO: Full menu available for carryout.
Curbside and contactless pick up. Delivery not available.

SCAN FOR MENU

SOME BASICS

Reservations:	YES
Spirits:	FULL BAR
Parking:	STREET/GARAGE
Outdoor Dining:	YES

CONNOR'S STEAKHOUSE

3501 South Tamiami Trail
941-260-3232
connorsrestaurant.com

SOUTHGATE	STEAKHOUSE	COST: $$$

HOURS: Sun-Thur, 11AM to 10PM
Fri & Sat, 11AM to 11PM

WHAT TO EXPECT: Lots of parking • Large menu
Lots of wines by the glass • OpenTable Reservations

CARRYOUT/DELIVERY INFO: Full menu available for carryout
and delivery. Curbside and contactless pick up. Delivery available
through Grubhub and Uber Eats.

SOME BASICS

SCAN FOR MENU

Reservations:	YES
Spirits:	FULL BAR
Parking:	LOT/VALET
Outdoor Dining:	YES

THE COTTAGE

153 Avenida Messina
941-312-9300
cottagesiestakey.com

SIESTA KEY	AMERICAN	COST: $$

HOURS: Mon-Thur, 12PM to 10PM • Fri & Sun, 11AM to 11PM

WHAT TO EXPECT: Tapas • Siesta Village • Outdoor dining
Vacation atmosphere

CARRYOUT/DELIVERY INFO: Full menu is available for carryout.
Delivery not available.

SOME BASICS

SCAN FOR MENU

Reservations:	NO
Spirits:	FULL BAR
Parking:	STREET/VALET
Outdoor Dining:	YES

CRAB & FIN

420 St. Armands Circle
941-388-3964
crabfinrestaurant.com

ST. ARMANDS	SEAFOOD	COST: $$$

HOURS: Sun-Thur, 11:30AM to 10PM
Fri & Sat, 11:30AM to 10:30PM

WHAT TO EXPECT: Great for a date • Sunday brunch
Online reservations • Early dining options

CARRYOUT/DELIVERY INFO: Full menu available for carryout.
Curbside and contactless pick up. Delivery not available.

SCAN FOR MENU

SOME BASICS

Reservations:	YES
Spirits:	FULL BAR
Parking:	STREET/LOT
Outdoor Dining:	YES

THE CROW'S NEST

1968 Tarpon Center Drive
941-484-9551
crowsnest-venice.com

VENICE	SEAFOOD	COST: $$

HOURS: Lunch, Daily 11:30AM to 3PM
Sun-Thur, 4:30PM to 8PM • Fri & Sat, 5:30PM to 8:30PM

WHAT TO EXPECT: Water view • Good wine list
OpenTable Reservations

CARRYOUT/DELIVERY INFO: Full menu available for carryout.
Curbside and contactless pick up. Delivery available through
Uber Eats.

SCAN FOR MENU

SOME BASICS

Reservations:	YES
Spirits:	FULL BAR
Parking:	LOT
Outdoor Dining:	YES

CURRY STATION

3550 Clark Road
941-924-7222
currystation.net

DOWNTOWN	INDIAN	COST: $$

HOURS: Lunch Buffet: Mon-Sat, 11:30AM to 2:30PM
Dinner: Mon-Sat, 5PM to 9:30PM • CLOSED SUNDAY

WHAT TO EXPECT: Huge Indian menu • Lots of curries
A dozen naan and other breads • Online reservations

CARRYOUT/DELIVERY INFO: Full menu available for carryout.
Curbside pick up. Delivery available through Bite Squad, Uber
Eats, Grubhub and DoorDash.

SCAN FOR MENU

SOME BASICS

Reservations:	YES
Spirits:	BEER/WINE
Parking:	LOT
Outdoor Dining:	NO

DAIQUIRI DECK RAW BAR

5250 Ocean Boulevard*
941-349-8697
daiquirideck.com

SIESTA KEY	AMERICAN	COST: $$

HOURS: Sun-Thur, 11AM to 11PM • Fri & Sat, 11AM to 1AM

WHAT TO EXPECT: Great after beach stop • Super casual
Good for families • Good for groups

CARRYOUT/DELIVERY INFO: Online ordering available. Most
menu items available for carryout. Curbside and contactless pick
up. Delivery not available.

SCAN FOR MENU

SOME BASICS

Reservations:	NO
Spirits:	FULL BAR
Parking:	STREET
Outdoor Dining:	YES

DARUMA JAPANESE STEAK HOUSE

5459 Fruitville Road*
941-342-6600
darumarestaurant.com

FRUITVILLE RD	ASIAN	COST: $$

HOURS: Daily, 4PM to 10PM

WHAT TO EXPECT: Fun date night • Good for kids • Great for groups
Private parties

CARRYOUT/DELIVERY INFO: Full menu available for carryout and delivery. Delivery through Bite Squad, DoorDash, Grubhub and Uber Eats.

SCAN FOR MENU

SOME BASICS
Reservations:	YES
Spirits:	FULL BAR
Parking:	LOT
Outdoor Dining:	NO

DARWIN EVOLUTIONARY CUISINE

4141 South Tamiami Trail
941-260-5964
chefdarwin.com

SOUTH TRAIL	PERUVIAN	COST: $$

HOURS: Tue-Thur, 12PM to 8PM • Fri & Sat, 12PM to 9PM
CLOSED SUNDAY & MONDAY

WHAT TO EXPECT: Happy Hour specials • Lots of parking
Fun for a group • Authentic Peruvian cuisine

CARRYOUT/DELIVERY INFO: Full menu available for carryout.
Curbside pick up. Delivery not available.

SCAN FOR MENU

SOME BASICS
Reservations:	YES
Spirits:	FULL BAR
Parking:	LOT
Outdoor Dining:	NO

DEMETRIO'S PIZZERIA
4410 South Tamiami Trail
941-922-1585
www.demetriospizzeria.com

SOUTH TRAIL	PIZZA	COST: $$

HOURS: Daily, 11AM to 8PM

WHAT TO EXPECT: Good for kids • Easy on the wallet
Catering available • In business 40+ years

CARRYOUT/DELIVERY INFO: Full menu available for carryout and
delivery. Delivery through Bite Squad.

SCAN FOR MENU

SOME BASICS
Reservations:	NO
Spirits:	BEER/WINE
Parking:	LOT
Outdoor Dining:	NO

DER DUTCHMAN
3713 Bahia Vista Street
941-955-8007
dhgroup.com

PINECRAFT	AMISH	COST: $$

HOURS: Mon-Thur, 6AM to 8PM • Fri & Sat, 6AM to 9PM
CLOSED SUNDAY

WHAT TO EXPECT: Good for kids • Easy on the wallet
Home cooking • Great pie • Groups welcome

CARRYOUT/DELIVERY INFO: Full menu available for carryout and
delivery. Curbside pick up for carryout. Delivery through Grubhub.

SCAN FOR MENU

SOME BASICS
Reservations:	NO
Spirits:	NONE
Parking:	LOT
Outdoor Dining:	NO

DOLCE ITALIA

6551 Gateway Avenue
941-921-7007
dolceitaliarestaurant.com

GULF GATE	ITALIAN	COST: $$

HOURS: Mon-Thur, 5PM to 9PM • Fri & Sat, 5PM to 9:30PM
CLOSED SUNDAY

WHAT TO EXPECT: Great for a date • Good wine list
Lots of atmosphere • Family owned

CARRYOUT/DELIVERY INFO: Full menu available for carryout.
Delivery not available.

SCAN FOR MENU

SOME BASICS

Reservations:	YES
Spirits:	BEER/WINE
Parking:	LOT
Outdoor Dining:	NO

DRIFT KITCHEN

700 Benjamin Franklin Drive (Lido Beach Resort)
941-388-2161
www.lidobeachresort.com/dining/drift

LIDO KEY	AMERICAN	COST: $$

HOURS: Daily, 7AM to 10PM

WHAT TO EXPECT: Upscale dining • Great gulf views
Lido Beach Resort

CARRYOUT/DELIVERY INFO: Full menu available for carryout.
Phone-in only. Delivery not available.

SCAN FOR MENU

SOME BASICS

Reservations:	YES
Spirits:	FULL BAR
Parking:	LOT
Outdoor Dining:	NO

DRUNKEN POET CAFÉ

1572 Main Street
941-955-8404
drunkenpoetcafesrq.com

DOWNTOWN	THAI	COST: $$

HOURS: Sun-Thur, 11AM to 10PM • Fri & Sat, 11AM to 12AM

WHAT TO EXPECT: Casual atmosphere • Good vegan options
OpenTable reservations • Great for small groups

CARRYOUT/DELIVERY INFO: Online ordering available. Full menu available for carryout. Delivery through ChowNow, Bite Squad and Postmates.

SCAN FOR MENU

SOME BASICS

Reservations:	YES
Spirits:	BEER/WINE
Parking:	STREET
Outdoor Dining:	YES

DRY DOCK WATERFRONT RESTAURANT

412 Gulf of Mexico Drive
941-383-0102
drydockwaterfrontgrill.com

LONGBOAT KEY	SEAFOOD	COST: $$

HOURS: Sun-Thur, 11AM to 9PM • Fri & Sat, 11AM to 10PM

WHAT TO EXPECT: Great water view • Local seafood • Happy Hour
Good for groups • OpenTable reservations

CARRYOUT/DELIVERY INFO: Full menu available for carryout. Phone-in orders only. Delivery not available.

SCAN FOR MENU

SOME BASICS

Reservations:	YES
Spirits:	FULL BAR
Parking:	LOT
Outdoor Dining:	YES

Artichokes Esther-Style

Chef Paul Mattison

My grandmother, Esther, never believed in throwing anything away. Once the artichoke hearts were dipped in the egg wash and cooked in olive oil, she would scramble the leftover egg wash in the same skillet, creating slightly green eggs. The two served together was truly Esther-Style. - Chef Paul Mattison

INGREDIENTS
12 artichoke hearts
½ cup flour
3 eggs
1 Tbsp water
½ cup flour
½ cup grated Parmesan cheese
½ cup olive oil

METHOD
Halve, rinse and drain artichoke hearts. Dredge in flour then dip in an egg wash made by whisking the eggs with the water. Combine the remaining flour with the Parmesan cheese and dredge the artichoke hearts again, shaking off excess coating. Pour oil into a large skillet and preheat to medium-high. Add artichokes, cut side down first, and pan fry for 2 minutes. Turn and cook for 2 more minutes until golden brown. Serve with Piccata Sauce and garnish with chopped basil and grated Parmesan cheese.

PICCATA SAUCE ESTHER-STYLE

INGREDIENTS
1½ Tbsp olive oil
4 tsp finely diced shallots

2 Tbsp capers
2 tsp chopped garlic
1 cup white wine
4 Tbsp butter
2 Tbsp seeded, diced tomatoes
10 chiffonade medium basil leaves
2 Tbsp grated Parmesan cheese
Juice of 1 lemon
Salt and pepper to taste

METHOD
Preheat olive oil in a sauté pan to medium-low. Add shallots and cook 2 to 3 minutes until soft. Add capers and garlic and cook for one minute. Add wine, increase heat to high and reduce by half. Reduce heat and add butter. Once melted, add tomatoes, basil, cheese and lemon juice. Season to taste.

Serves 1 (or shareable for 2)

Chef Paul Mattison, executive chef and proprietor of Mattison's, operates a successful culinary group on Florida's Gulf Coast.

DUTCH VALLEY RESTAURANT
6721 South Tamiami Trail
941-924-1770
dutchvalleyrestaurant.net

SOUTH TRAIL	AMERICAN	COST: $$

HOURS: Daily, 7AM to 9PM

WHAT TO EXPECT: Comfort food • Casual dining • Broasted Chicken! Good for kids • Early dining crowd

CARRYOUT/DELIVERY INFO: Full menu is available for carryout. Curbside and contactless pick up available. Delivery not available.

SOME BASICS

SCAN FOR MENU

Reservations:	NO
Spirits:	BEER/WINE
Parking:	LOT
Outdoor Dining:	NO

DUVAL'S FRESH. LOCAL. SEAFOOD.

1435 Main Street
941-312-4001
duvalsfreshlocalseafood.com

DOWNTOWN	AMERICAN	COST: $$$

HOURS: Mon-Thur, 11AM to 10PM • Fri & Sat, 11AM to 11PM
Sun, 11AM to 10PM

WHAT TO EXPECT: Brunch • OpenTable reservations
Great Happy Hour • Free shuttle to the restaurant

CARRYOUT/DELIVERY INFO: Online ordering. Full menu available for carryout and delivery. Curbside and contactless pick up. Delivery through Bite Squad, Uber Eats and DoorDash.

SCAN FOR MENU

SOME BASICS

Reservations:	YES
Spirits:	FULL BAR
Parking:	STREET
Outdoor Dining:	YES

EL TORO BRAVO

3218 Clark Road
941-924-0006
eltorobravosarasota.com

	MEXICAN	COST: $$

HOURS: Mon-Thur, 11AM to 8PM • Fri & Sat, 11AM to 9PM
CLOSED SUNDAY

WHAT TO EXPECT: Great for families • Super casual dining
Usually busy • Online reservations • Lots of parking

CARRYOUT/DELIVERY INFO: Full menu available for carryout. Curbside and contactless pick up. Delivery available through Bite Squad, Grubhub and DoorDash.

SCAN FOR MENU

SOME BASICS

Reservations:	YES
Spirits:	BEER/WINE
Parking:	LOT
Outdoor Dining:	NO

EUPHEMIA HAYE

5540 Gulf of Mexico Drive
941-383-3633
euphemiahaye.com

LONGBOAT KEY	AMERICAN	COST: $$$$

HOURS: Wed-Sun, 6PM to 8:30PM • Curbside starts at 4:30PM
CLOSED MONDAY & TUESDAY

WHAT TO EXPECT: Great for a date • Online reservations
Fine dining experience • Great for special occasions

CARRYOUT/DELIVERY INFO: Most menu items available for carryout. Curbside, contactless pick up available for carryout. Delivery not available.

SOME BASICS

Reservations:	YES
Spirits:	FULL BAR
Parking:	LOT
Outdoor Dining:	NO

SCAN FOR MENU

EVOQ

100 Marina View Drive (Westin Sarasota)
941-260-8255
evoqsarasota.com

DOWTOWN	AMERICAN	COST: $$$

HOURS: Lunch & Dinner Daily

WHAT TO EXPECT: Handmade cocktail selections • Good wine list
Upscale comfort food • OpenTable reservations

CARRYOUT/DELIVERY INFO: Phone-in for carryout. Full menu available for carryout. No curbside or contactless pick up. Delivery not available.

SOME BASICS

Reservations:	YES
Spirits:	FULL BAR
Parking:	Valet
Outdoor Dining:	NO

SCAN FOR MENU

1592 WOOD FIRED KITCHEN & COCKTAILS `NEW`

1592 Main Street
941-365-2234
1592srq.com

DOWNTOWN	GREEK	COST: $$

HOURS: Mon-Thur, 11AM to 9PM • Fri & Sat, 11AM to 10PM
CLOSED SUNDAY

WHAT TO EXPECT: Great casual dining • Online reservations
Nice street-side dining • Good downtown lunch spot

CARRYOUT/DELIVERY INFO: Full menu available for carryout.
Curbside and contactless pick up. Limited menu available for
delivery. Delivery through Bite Squad, Uber Eats and Grubhub.

SCAN FOR MENU

SOME BASICS

Reservations:	YES
Spirits:	BEER/WINE
Parking:	STREET
Outdoor Dining:	YES

FINS AT SHARKEY'S

1600 Harbor Drive South
941-999-3467
finsatsharkys.com

VENICE	AMERICAN	COST: $$$

HOURS: Lunch, Daily, 12PM to 3PM
Dinner, Daily, 4PM to 10PM

WHAT TO EXPECT: Beachfront dining • Online reservations
Good wine list • "Steakhouse with a Serious Seafood Side"

CARRYOUT/DELIVERY INFO: Limited menu available for carryout.
Curbside pick up. Delivery not available.

SCAN FOR MENU

SOME BASICS

Reservations:	YES
Spirits:	FULL BAR
Parking:	LOT
Outdoor Dining:	YES

FLAVIO'S BRICK OVEN AND BAR

5239 Ocean Boulevard
941-349-0995
flaviosbrickovenandbar.com

SIESTA KEY	ITALIAN	COST: $$$

HOURS: Sun-Thur 4PM to 10PM • Fri & Sat, 4PM to 10:30PM

WHAT TO EXPECT: Homemade Italian cuisine • Brick oven pizza
Good meetup spot • Siesta Village location

CARRYOUT/DELIVERY INFO: Full menu available for carryout.
Curbside and contactless pick up. Delivery through DoorDash.

SOME BASICS

Reservations: YES
Spirits: FULL BAR
Parking: LOT
Outdoor Dining: YES

SCAN FOR MENU

Now It's Easy To
Keep Up With All Of Your
Sarasota Food News & Happenings

Find, Like and Follow
dineSarasota

FLAVIO'S ON MAIN

NEW

1766 Main Street
941-960-2305
flaviosbrickovenandbar.com

DOWNTOWN	ITALIAN	COST: $$$

HOURS: Sun-Thur 4PM to 10PM • Fri & Sat, 4PM to 10:30PM

WHAT TO EXPECT: Casual Italian • Good wine list
Happy Hour specials

CARRYOUT/DELIVERY INFO: Full menu available for carryout.
Curbside and contactless pick up. Delivery through DoorDash.

SCAN FOR MENU

SOME BASICS
Reservations:	YES
Spirits:	FULL BAR
Parking:	STREET
Outdoor Dining:	YES

FRESH CATCH FISH MARKET & GRILL

NEW

7119 South Tamiami Trail
941-413-7133
freshcatchfishmarketandgrill.com

SOUTH TRAIL	SEAFOOD	COST: $$

HOURS: Mon-Sat, 11AM to 8PM • CLOSED SUNDAY

WHAT TO EXPECT: Fish market + restaurant • Lots of parking
Small and casual dining space

CARRYOUT/DELIVERY INFO: Full menu available for carryout.
Curbside pick up. Delivery not available.

SCAN FOR MENU

SOME BASICS
Reservations:	YES
Spirits:	BEER/WINE
Parking:	LOT
Outdoor Dining:	NO

FRESH START CAFE

630 South Orange Avenue
941-373-1242
freshstartcafesrq.com

BURNS COURT	AMERICAN	COST: $$

HOURS: Thur-Tue, 9AM to 2PM • CLOSED WEDNESDAY

WHAT TO EXPECT: Breakfast & lunch spot • Casual dining

CARRYOUT/DELIVERY INFO: Full menu available for carryout.
Phone-in orders only. Curbside and contactless pick up available.
Delivery not available.

SCAN FOR MENU

SOME BASICS
Reservations: NO
Spirits: NONE
Parking: STREET
Outdoor Dining: NO

FUSHIPOKÉ

128 North Orange Avenue
941-330-1795
fushipoke.com

DOWTOWN	ASIAN	COST: $$

HOURS: Mon-Sat, 11AM to 8PM • CLOSED SUNDAY

WHAT TO EXPECT: Good for families • Super causal
Good for a quick lunch • Friendly service

CARRYOUT/DELIVERY INFO: Online ordering. Full menu available
for carryout. Curbside pick up. Delivery through Grubhub.

SCAN FOR MENU

SOME BASICS
Reservations: NONE
Spirits: BEER/WINE
Parking: STREET
Outdoor Dining: NO

GECKO'S GRILL & PUB

6606 South Tamiami Trail*
941-248-2020
geckosgrill.com

SOUTH TRAIL	AMERICAN	COST: $$

HOURS: Daily, 11AM to 10PM

WHAT TO EXPECT: Great to watch a game • Yelp waitlist
Good burgers • "American Pub Food"

CARRYOUT/DELIVERY INFO: Online ordering. Curbside and contactless pick up. Delivery through Bite Squad.

SCAN FOR MENU

SOME BASICS

Reservations:	NO
Spirits:	FULL BAR
Parking:	LOT
Outdoor Dining:	YES

GENTILE BROTHERS CHEESESTEAKS

7523 South Tamiami Trail
941-926-0441
gentilesteaks.com

SOUTH TRAIL	AMERICAN	COST: $

HOURS: Mon-Sat, 11AM to 7PM • CLOSED SUNDAY

WHAT TO EXPECT: Philly experience • No frills dining
Easy on the wallet • Family owned • Good for kids

CARRYOUT/DELIVERY INFO: Full menu available for carryout. Curbside pick up available. Delivery through Uber Eats, Bite Squad and DoorDash.

SCAN FOR MENU

SOME BASICS

Reservations:	NO
Spirits:	NONE
Parking:	LOT
Outdoor Dining:	NO

BURGER TIME!
SOME OF SARASOTA'S BEST

Hob Nob Drive-In • 1701 N. Washington Blvd. • 955-5001
WHAT TO EXPECT: Always one of Sarasota's best burger stops. Old school, nothing fancy. The "Hob Nob" burger basket is a must.

Indigenous • 239 S. Links Ave. • 706-4740
WHAT TO EXPECT: This one is always a pleasant surprise. Chef Phelps puts out a delicious burger. Can you say, bacon jam?

Island House Tap & Grill • 5110 Ocean Blvd. • 487-8116
WHAT TO EXPECT: They have a super secret prep method that turns out a perfectly cooked, juicy, and delicious burger every time!

Knick's Tavern & Grill • 1818 S. Osprey Ave. • 955-7761
WHAT TO EXPECT: Known for their burgers. Big and super tasty. For something a little different try a "Brunch Burger." Yep, egg topper.

Made • 1990 Main St. • 953-2900
WHAT TO EXPECT: Niman Ranch beef + billionaire bacon. What more do you really need to say? Delicious! Great sides, too.

Patrick's 1481 • 1481 Main St. • 955-1481
WHAT TO EXPECT: It's all about the burger at Patrick's. This restaurant is a downtown institution. Try it and you'll know why.

Shake Shack • 190 N. Cattlemen Rd. • 413-1351
WHAT TO EXPECT: If you have a Shake Shack in your town/city it has to make your "best of" list. Nothing quite like a ShackBurger.

Shakespeare's • 3550 S. Osprey Ave. • 364-5938
WHAT TO EXPECT: A caramelized onion & Brie burger! English pub atmosphere. Lots and lots of craft beer to wash it all down.

Tasty Home Cookin' • 3854 S. Tuttle Ave. • 921-4969
WHAT TO EXPECT: This one is just a bit different in the burger department. Think White Castle. 3 "Tasty Burgers" for $3.79!!

GILLIGAN'S ISLAND BAR
5253 Ocean Boulevard
941-346-8122
gilligansislandbar.com

SIESTA KEY	AMERICAN	COST: $$

HOURS: Sun-Thur, 11AM to 11PM • Fri & Sat, 11AM to 12AM

WHAT TO EXPECT: Siesta Village • Live music • Younger crowd
Fun weekend hangout place

CARRYOUT/DELIVERY INFO: Full menu available for carryout.
Delivery not available.

SCAN FOR MENU

SOME BASICS
Reservations:	NO
Spirits:	FULL BAR
Parking:	STREET
Outdoor Dining:	YES

THE GRASSHOPPER
7253 South Tamiami Trail
941-923-3688
thegrasshoppertexmex.com

SOUTH TRAIL	MEXICAN	COST: $$

HOURS: Mon-Thur, 11AM to 9:30PM • Fri & Sat, 11AM to 10PM
CLOSED SUNDAY • Happy Hour, 3:30PM to 6:30PM

WHAT TO EXPECT: Easy on the wallet • Happy Hour
Good cocktail selection • Good for groups

CARRYOUT/DELIVERY INFO: Online ordering available. Curbside
and contactless pick up. Delivery through ChowNow.

SCAN FOR MENU

SOME BASICS
Reservations:	YES
Spirits:	FULL BAR
Parking:	LOT
Outdoor Dining:	NO

GRILLSMITH

6240 South Tamiami Trail
941-259-8383
www.grillsmith.com

SOUTH TRAIL	AMERICAN	COST: $$

HOURS: Mon-Thur, 4PM to 9PM • Fri, 4PM to 9:30PM
Sat, 11AM to 9:30PM • Sun, 11AM to 9PM

WHAT TO EXPECT: Upscale casual • Plenty of parking
Good Happy Hour • Online reservations

CARRYOUT/DELIVERY INFO: Online ordering. Full menu available for carryout and delivery. Curbside pick up. Delivery through Uber Eats, Grubhub and Postmates.

SCAN FOR MENU

SOME BASICS

Reservations:	YES
Spirits:	FULL BAR
Parking:	LOT
Outdoor Dining:	NO

GROVE

10670 Boardwalk Loop
941-893-4321
grovelwr.com

LAKEWOOD RANCH	AMERICAN	COST: $$$

HOURS: Mon-Thur, 11:30AM to 10PM • Fri, 11:30AM to 10:30PM
Sat, 8AM to 10:30PM • 8AM to 10PM

WHAT TO EXPECT: Happy Hour • Culinary cocktails
Weekend brunch • OpenTable reservations

CARRYOUT/DELIVERY INFO: Online ordering. Full menu available for carryout or delivery. Curbside pick up. Free delivery available.

SCAN FOR MENU

SOME BASICS

Reservations:	YES
Spirits:	FULL BAR
Parking:	LOT
Outdoor Dining:	YES

GULF GATE FOOD & BEER
6528 Superior Avenue*
941-952-3361
eatfooddrinkbeer.com

GULF GATE	AMERICAN	COST: $$

HOURS: Mon-Thur, 11AM to 1AM • Fri, 11AM to 2AM
Sat, 10AM to 2AM • Sun, 10AM to 1AM

WHAT TO EXPECT: Super casual • Good local beer selection
Later night menu • Sat. & Sun. brunch

CARRYOUT/DELIVERY INFO: Full menu is available for carryout.
No curbside pick up. Delivery through Bite Squad.

SCAN FOR MENU

SOME BASICS
Reservations:	NO
Spirits:	BEER/WINE
Parking:	STREET/LOT
Outdoor Dining:	NO

HARRY'S CONTINENTAL KITCHENS
525 St. Judes Drive
941-383-0777
harryskitchen.com

LONGBOAT KEY	AMERICAN	COST: $$$

HOURS: Restaurant - Daily, 9AM to 9PM
Deli - 11AM to 7PM

WHAT TO EXPECT: Great for a date • Longboat Key
Upscale Florida dining

CARRYOUT/DELIVERY INFO: Full menu available for carryout.
Curbside and contactless pick up. Delivery not available.

SCAN FOR MENU

SOME BASICS
Reservations:	YES
Spirits:	FULL BAR
Parking:	LOT
Outdoor Dining:	YES

HOB NOB DRIVE-IN RESTAURANT

1701 North Washington Boulevard (301 & 17th St.)
941-955-5001
hobnobdrivein.com

DOWNTOWN	AMERICAN	COST: $

HOURS: Mon-Sat, 7AM to 8PM • Sun, 8AM to 4PM

WHAT TO EXPECT: Easy on the wallet • Fun! • Great for kids
Sarasota's oldest drive-in. • Great burger!

CARRYOUT/DELIVERY INFO: Full menu available for carryout.
Curbside and contactless pick up available. Delivery not
available.

SOME BASICS

SCAN FOR MENU

Reservations:	NO
Spirits:	BEER/WINE
Parking:	LOT
Outdoor Dining:	YES

THE HUB BAJA GRILL

5148 Ocean Boulevard
941-349-6800
thehubsiestakey.com

SIESTA KEY	AMERICAN	COST: $$

HOURS: Sun-Thur, 11AM to 10PM • Fri & Sat, 11AM to 11PM

WHAT TO EXPECT: Island dining experience • Good for families
Busy in season • Live music daily

CARRYOUT/DELIVERY INFO: Full menu available for carryout.
Phone-in orders only. Delivery not available.

SOME BASICS

SCAN FOR MENU

Reservations:	NO
Spirits:	FULL BAR
Parking:	STREET
Outdoor Dining:	YES

ICHIBAN SUSHI

2724 Stickney Point Road
941-924-1611
sarasotaichiban.com

SUSHI	COST: $$

HOURS: Mon-Fri, 11AM to 2PM • Mon-Fri, 4:30PM to 9:30PM
Sat, 4PM to 9:30PM • CLOSED SUNDAY

WHAT TO EXPECT: All you can eat sushi • Casual atmosphere
Family friendly • Lots of parking

CARRYOUT/DELIVERY INFO: Full menu (+ special combos
carryout only) available for carryout. Curbside pick up. Delivery
through Uber Eats, DoorDash, Bite Squad and Grubhub.

SCAN FOR MENU

SOME BASICS

Reservations:	YES
Spirits:	FULL BAR
Parking:	LOT
Outdoor Dining:	NO

IL PANIFICIO

1703 Main Street*
941-921-5570
panificiousa.com

DOWNTOWN	ITALIAN	COST: $$

HOURS: Daily, 10AM to 9PM

WHAT TO EXPECT: Great for lunch • Easy on the wallet • Quick
Good for kids

CARRYOUT/DELIVERY INFO: Online ordering. Full menu available
for carryout and delivery. Delivery through Bite Squad, DoorDash
and Slice.

SCAN FOR MENU

SOME BASICS

Reservations:	NO
Spirits:	BEER/WINE
Parking:	STREET
Outdoor Dining:	YES

INDIGENOUS RESTAURANT

239 South Links Avenue
941-706-4740
indigenoussarasota.com

TOWLES CT	AMERICAN	COST: $$$

HOURS: Tues-Sat, 5PM to 9PM • CLOSED SUNDAY & MONDAY

WHAT TO EXPECT: Great for a date • Fine dining, casual feel
Towles Court neighborhood • Limited outdoor seating

CARRYOUT/DELIVERY INFO: Carryout available. Special, rotating menu. Limited outdoor and indoor seating. Delivery not available.

SOME BASICS

SCAN FOR MENU

Reservations:	YES
Spirits:	BEER/WINE
Parking:	LOT/STREET
Outdoor Dining:	YES

INKAWASI PERUVIAN RESTAURANT

10667 Boardwalk Loop
941-360-1110
inkawasirestaurant.com

LAKEWOOD RANCH	PERUVIAN	COST: $$

HOURS: Mon, Wed-Thur & Sun, 12PM to 9PM
Tue, 5PM to 9PM • Sat, 12PM to 11PM

WHAT TO EXPECT: Casual dining atmosphere • Tapas Happy Hour
Lakewood Ranch Main Street location

CARRYOUT/DELIVERY INFO: Full menu available for carryout and delivery. Curbside and contactless pick up. Delivery through Bite Squad and Grubhub.

SOME BASICS

SCAN FOR MENU

Reservations:	YES
Spirits:	BEER/WINE
Parking:	LOT/STREET
Outdoor Dining:	NO

VEGETARIAN?
SARASOTA'S BEST PLACES

Vegetarian and vegan lifestyles both offer a healthy way of eating. But, as any one who keeps either of these diets knows, dining out can sometimes be more than a challenge. I mean, how many grilled cheese sandwiches can one person consume? Don't despair. We're here to help. Sarasota has its share of options for those who choose a meat-free existence. Keep in mind that the places listed below may not be strictly vegan/veg only. But, they will offer some nice menu options.

Leaf & Lentil • 2801 N. Tamiami Trl. • 413-5685
THE HIGHLIGHTS: Lots of great variety. Vegan/veg, fast casual restaurant. Small plate and main plate options.

Lila • 1576 Main St. • 296-1042
THE HIGHLIGHTS: Named one of the best vegetarian restaurants in the country by OpenTable. Refined vegetarian cuisine.

Screaming Goat Taqueria • 6606 Superior Ave. • 210-3992
THE HIGHLIGHTS: Tacos, bowls, and more. Lots of vegan/veg options here. Your non-veg friends will be super happy, too!

Spice Station • 1438 Boulevard of the Arts • 343-2894
THE HIGHLIGHTS: Fantastic Thai cuisine. They've got a large section of vegetarian dishes on their menu. Cozy dining space.

Tsunami Sushi • 100 Central Ave. • 366-1033
THE HIGHLIGHTS: There are lots of sushi options in town. Tsunami has an entire menu of vegan sushi rolls. Lots of creativity here.

Veg • 6538 Gateway Ave. • 312-6424
THE HIGHLIGHTS: The name says it best. Vegetarian + seafood. Dozens of their dishes can be made vegan too. Delicious!

IRISH 31

3750 South Tamiami Trail
941-234-9265
irish31.com

SOUTH TRAIL	IRISH	COST: $$

HOURS: Mon, 3PM to 11PM • Tue-Thur, 12PM to 11PM
Fri & Sat, 12PM to 12AM • Sun, 12PM to 10PM

WHAT TO EXPECT: Lots of parking • Good for a game
Vibrant atmosphere • Daily specials • Happy Hour

CARRYOUT/DELIVERY INFO: Online ordering available. Full menu available for carryout. Limited menu is available for delivery. Delivery through Uber Eats.

SCAN FOR MENU

SOME BASICS

Reservations:	NO
Spirits:	FULL BAR
Parking:	LOT
Outdoor Dining:	YES

ISLAND HOUSE TAP & GRILL

5110 Ocean Boulevard
941-487-8116
islandhousetapandgrill.com

SIESTA KEY	AMERICAN	COST: $$

HOURS: Daily, 12PM to 10AM

WHAT TO EXPECT: Great craft beers • Fantastic burgers & tacos
Outdoor patio • Local favorite • Daily specials

CARRYOUT/DELIVERY INFO: Full menu is available for carryout and delivery. Curbside pick up. Delivery through Bite Squad, DoorDash, Uber Eats and Grubhub.

SCAN FOR MENU

SOME BASICS

Reservations:	NONE
Spirits:	BEER/WINE
Parking:	LOT
Outdoor Dining:	YES

JACK DUSTY

1111 Ritz-Carlton Drive
941-309-2266
ritzcarlton.com/en/hotels/florida/sarasota/dining/jack-dusty

DOWNTOWN	SEAFOOD	COST: $$$

HOURS: Breakfast, lunch, and dinner daily

WHAT TO EXPECT: Walking distance to downtown • Water view
Handmade cocktails • OpenTable reservations

CARRYOUT/DELIVERY INFO: Full menu available for carryout.
Delivery not available.

SCAN FOR MENU

SOME BASICS

Reservations:	YES
Spirits:	FULL BAR
Parking:	VALET
Outdoor Dining:	YES

JPAN RESTAURANT & SUSHI BAR

3800 South Tamiami Trail (Shops at Siesta Row)*
941-954-5726
jpanrestaurant.com

SHOPS AT SIESTA ROW	JAPANESE	COST: $$

HOURS: Lunch, Mon-Fri, 11:30AM to 2PM
Dinner nightly from 5PM to 9PM

WHAT TO EXPECT: Great for a date • Big sushi menu
Great lunch combos • OpenTable reservations

CARRYOUT/DELIVERY INFO: Online ordering. Curbside and
contactless pick up. Delivery through Bite Squad, Grubhub
and DoorDash.

SCAN FOR MENU

SOME BASICS

Reservations:	YES
Spirits:	BEER/WINE
Parking:	LOT
Outdoor Dining:	YES

JR'S OLD PACKINGHOUSE CAFE
987 South Packinghouse Drive
941-371-9358
packinghousecafe.com

AMERICAN	COST: $$

HOURS: Mon-Thur, 11AM to 9PM • Fri & Sat, 11AM to 10PM
Sun, 12PM to 6PM

WHAT TO EXPECT: Fun for a date • LIVE music
Great burgers & Cuban sandwiches

CARRYOUT/DELIVERY INFO: Full menu available for carryout and
delivery. Curbside, contactless pick up. Delivery through
Bite Squad.

SOME BASICS

SCAN FOR MENU

Reservations:	NO
Spirits:	FULL BAR
Parking:	LOT
Outdoor Dining:	YES

KACEY'S SEAFOOD & MORE
4904 Fruitville Road
941-378-3644
kaceysseafood.com

FRUITVILLE RD	SEAFOOD	COST: $$

HOURS: Tue-Sun, 11AM to 8PM • CLOSED MONDAY

WHAT TO EXPECT: Good for families • Casual dining
Lots of parking

CARRYOUT/DELIVERY INFO: Online ordering. Curbside pick up
available. Delivery through DoorDash.

SOME BASICS

SCAN FOR MENU

Reservations:	NONE
Spirits:	BEER/WINE
Parking:	LOT
Online Menu:	YES

KARL EHMER'S ALPINE STEAKHOUSE

4520 South Tamiami Trail
941-922-3797
alpinesteak.com

SOUTH TRAIL	AMERICAN	COST: $$

HOURS: Mon to Sat, 9AM to 8PM
CLOSED SUNDAY

WHAT TO EXPECT: Great butcher shop • Home of the "TurDucKen" German cuisine • Featured on the Food Network

CARRYOUT/DELIVERY INFO: Full menu available for carryout and delivery. Curbside and contactless pick up. Delivery available through DoorDash.

SCAN FOR MENU

SOME BASICS

Reservations:	NO
Spirits:	FULL BAR
Parking:	LOT
Outdoor Dining:	NO

KIYOSHI SUSHI

6550 Gateway Avenue
941-924-3781

GULF GATE	SUSHI	COST: $$

HOURS: Tues-Thur, 5:30PM to 9PM • Fri & Sat, 5:30PM to 9:30PM
CLOSED SUNDAY & MONDAY

WHAT TO EXPECT: Traditional sushi • Casual & comfortable Beautiful presentations

CARRYOUT/DELIVERY INFO: ** *At press time, we were not able to verify the carryout and delivery options for this restaurant. We suggest you call for their most up to date information.* **

SCAN FOR MENU

SOME BASICS

Reservations:	YES
Spirits:	BEER/WINE
Parking:	STREET/LOT
Outdoor Dining:	NO

KNICK'S TAVERN & GRILL

1818 South Osprey Avenue
941-955-7761
knickstavernandgrill.com

SOUTHSIDE VILLAGE	AMERICAN	COST: $$

HOURS: Mon-Fri, 11:30AM to 10PM • Sat, 5PM to 10PM
CLOSED SUNDAY

WHAT TO EXPECT: Casual dining • Busy in season • Family owned
Local favorite • Great burgers & daily specials

CARRYOUT/DELIVERY INFO: Full menu available for carryout and delivery. Curbside pick up. Delivery through Uber Eats.

SCAN FOR MENU

SOME BASICS

Reservations:	YES
Spirits:	BEER/WINE
Parking:	STREET/VALET
Outdoor Dining:	YES

2021 SARASOTA FOOD EVENTS

FORKS & CORKS

WHEN: April 29th - May 3rd
WHAT: Sponsored by the Sarasota-Manatee Originals. Super popular food event! Wine dinners, seminars, AND the Grand Tasting. A must for Sarasota foodies. Tickets go very fast.
INFO: eatlikealocal.com/forksandcorks

FLORIDA WINEFEST & AUCTION

WHEN: April 8-12th
WHAT: This charity event has been providing needed help to local children's programs for over 30 years. The Grand Tasting Brunch and Charity Auction are fantastic events. Don't miss!
INFO: floridawinefest.org

SAVOR SARASOTA RESTAURANT WEEK

WHEN: June 1-14th
WHAT: This restaurant week spans TWO full weeks. It features lots of popular restaurants and showcases three course menus.
INFO: savorsarasota.com

LA DOLCE VITA

2704 Stickney Point Road
941-210-3631
ladolcevitasarasota.com

	ITALIAN	COST: $$$

HOURS: Tues-Sat, 5PM to 9PM
CLOSED SUNDAY & MONDAY

WHAT TO EXPECT: Quaint • Family owned • Personal attention

CARRYOUT/DELIVERY INFO: Full menu available for carryout. Curbside pick up. Delivery through Uber Eats and Grubhub.

SCAN FOR MENU

SOME BASICS

Reservations:	YES
Spirits:	BEER/WINE
Parking:	LOT
Outdoor Dining:	NO

THE LAZY LOBSTER

7602 North Lockwood Ridge Road*
941-351-5515
sarasotalazylobster.com

NORTH SARASOTA	SEAFOOD	COST: $$

HOURS: Tues-Sun, 4PM to 9PM • CLOSED MONDAY

WHAT TO EXPECT: Great casual seafood • Early bird menu

CARRYOUT/DELIVERY INFO: Online ordering available. Most menu items available for carryout. Curbside and contactless pick up. Delivery not available.

SCAN FOR MENU

SOME BASICS

Reservations:	YES
Spirits:	FULL BAR
Parking:	LOT
Outdoor Dining:	YES

LE COLONNE RISTORANTE
22 South Boulevard of the Presidents
941-388-4348
lecolonnerestaurant.com

ST. ARMANDS	ITALIAN	COST: $$

HOURS: Daily, 11AM to 10PM

WHAT TO EXPECT: Happy Hour • Casual, upscale dining
Busy during season • OpenTable reservations

CARRYOUT/DELIVERY INFO: Full menu available for carryout and delivery. Curbside and contactless pick up. Delivery through Uber Eats and Bite Squad.

SOME BASICS

SCAN FOR MENU

Reservations:	YES
Spirits:	FULL BAR
Parking:	LOT/STREET
Outdoor Dining:	YES

LIBBY'S NEIGHBORHOOD BRASSERIE
1917 South Osprey Avenue*
941-487-7300
libbysneighborhoodbrasserie.com

SOUTHSIDE VILLAGE	AMERICAN	COST: $$$

HOURS: Daily, 11AM to 9PM

WHAT TO EXPECT: Upscale dining experience • Good wine list
Busy bar scene • Reservations a must during season

CARRYOUT/DELIVERY INFO: Online ordering available. Full menu available for carryout and delivery. Curbside and contactless pick up. Delivery through Bite Squad, Uber Eats and DoorDash.

SOME BASICS

SCAN FOR MENU

Reservations:	YES
Spirits:	FULL BAR
Parking:	LOT/STREET
Outdoor Dining:	YES

LILA

1576 Main Street
941-296-1042
lilasrq.com

DOWNTOWN	AMERICAN	COST: $$

HOURS: Mon-Fri, 11AM to 9PM • Sat, 10:30AM to 9PM
CLOSED SUNDAY

WHAT TO EXPECT: Organic, locally sourced menu • Lighter fare
OpenTable reservations • Lots of veg/vegan options

CARRYOUT/DELIVERY INFO: Full menu available for carryout
and delivery. Curbside and contactless pick up. Delivery available
through Bite Squad.

SCAN FOR MENU

SOME BASICS

Reservations:	YES
Spirits:	BEER/WINE
Parking:	STREET
Outdoor Dining:	NO

LOBSTER POT

5157 Ocean Boulevard
941-349-2323
sarasotalobsterpot.com

SIESTA KEY	SEAFOOD	COST: $$

HOURS: Mon-Thur, 11:30AM to 9PM • Fri & Sat, 11:30AM to 9:30PM
CLOSED SUNDAY

WHAT TO EXPECT: Great for families • Lobster ++ • Siesta Village
Good for kids

CARRYOUT/DELIVERY INFO: Most menu items available for
carryout. Curbside pick up. Delivery not available.

SCAN FOR MENU

SOME BASICS

Reservations:	6 OR MORE
Spirits:	BEER/WINE
Parking:	VALET/STREET
Outdoor Dining:	YES

LOVELY SQUARE

NEW

6559 Gateway Avenue
941-724-2512
lovelysquareflorida.com

GULF GATE	AMERICAN	COST: $$

HOURS: Lunch - Daily, 8AM to 2PM
Dinner - Tue-Sat, 4PM to 8PM

WHAT TO EXPECT: Casual dining spot • Nice selection of crepes
Good for families

CARRYOUT/DELIVERY INFO: Full menu available for carryout.
Curbside pick up. Delivery not available.

SCAN FOR MENU

SOME BASICS

Reservations:	NO
Spirits:	BEER/WINE
Parking:	LOT
Outdoor Dining:	NO

MADE

1990 Main Street
941-953-2900
maderestaurant.com

DOWNTOWN	AMERICAN	COST: $$

HOURS: Tue-Fri, Lunch, 11:30AM to 2PM • Sun, 10AM to 2:30PM
Tue-Sat, Dinner, 5PM to 10PM • CLOSED MONDAY

WHAT TO EXPECT: Great for a date • Upscale, American cuisine
Chef driven menu

CARRYOUT/DELIVERY INFO: Online ordering available. Full menu
available for carryout. Curbside pick up. Delivery not available.

SCAN FOR MENU

SOME BASICS

Reservations:	YES
Spirits:	FULL BAR
Parking:	STREET/GARAGE
Outdoor Dining:	YES

MADEMOISELLE PARIS

8527 Cooper Creek Boulevard
941-355-2323
mademoiselleparisutc.com

LWR	FRENCH	COST: $$

HOURS: Mon & Tue, 7:45AM to 5PM • Wed-Sat, 7:45AM to 9PM
Sunday Brunch, 7:45AM to 3PM

WHAT TO EXPECT: Traditional French fare • Casual European dining
Tartines, omlettes and more!

CARRYOUT/DELIVERY INFO: Online ordering. Full menu available
for carryout and delivery. Curbside and contactless pick up.
Delivery available through Bite Squad and Uber Eats.

SCAN FOR MENU

SOME BASICS
Reservations:	YES
Spirits:	BEER/WINE
Parking:	LOT
Outdoor Dining:	NO

MADFISH GRILL
4059 Cattleman Road
941-377-3474
madfishgrill.com

	SEAFOOD	COST: $$

HOURS: Mon-Sat, 11:30AM to 9PM • Sun, 11AM to 8PM
Sunday Brunch, 11AM to 2PM

WHAT TO EXPECT: Good for families • Daily specials
Happy Hour bites menu • Sunday brunch menu

CARRYOUT/DELIVERY INFO: Online ordering available. Full menu
available for carryout and delivery. Curbside and contactless
pick up. Delivery available through Bite Squad.

SCAN FOR MENU

SOME BASICS
Reservations:	YES
Spirits:	FULL BAR
Parking:	LOT
Outdoor Dining:	YES

MADISON AVENUE CAFE & DELI

28 Boulevard of the Presidents
941-388-3354
madisoncafesarasota.com

DOWNTOWN	AMERICAN	COST: $$

HOURS: Daily, 8AM to 3PM

WHAT TO EXPECT: Great for a date • Sunday brunch
Lively atmosphere • Nice bar scene

CARRYOUT/DELIVERY INFO: Full menu available for carryout.
No delivery available.

SOME BASICS

Reservations:	NO
Spirits:	BEER/WINE
Parking:	STREET/GARAGE
Outdoor Dining:	YES

SCAN FOR MENU

MAIN BAR SANDWICH SHOP

1944 Main Street
941-955-8733
themainbar.com

DOWNTOWN	DELI	COST: $

HOURS: Mon-Sat, 10AM to 4PM • CLOSED SUNDAY

WHAT TO EXPECT: Great for quick lunch • Easy on the wallet
Lively atmosphere • Fantastic service

CARRYOUT/DELIVERY INFO: Most menu items available for
carryout and delivery. Delivery available through Uber Eats and
DoorDash.

SOME BASICS

Reservations:	NO
Spirits:	BEER/WINE
Parking:	STREET
Outdoor Dining:	NO

SCAN FOR MENU

SARASOTA MARKETS AND SPECIALTY STORES

A Taste of Europe • 2130 Gulf Gate Dr. • 921-9084
WHAT YOU CAN FIND THERE: Foods from twenty different European countries. Fresh deli, specialty cheeses, beer, wine, and more.

Artisan Cheese Company • 550 Central Ave. • 951-7860
WHAT YOU CAN FIND THERE: Cheese store. Hard to find small domestic dairies. Lunch menu. Classes. Knowledgeable staff.

Big Water Fish Market • 6641 Midnight Pass Rd. • 554-8101
WHAT YOU CAN FIND THERE: Fresh Florida fish. Great prepared seafood items. Just south of Siesta Key's south bridge.

The Butcher's Block • 3242 17th St. • 955-2822
WHAT YOU CAN FIND THERE: Meat market/butcher shop. Custom cuts, prime meats. Good wine selection. They have gift baskets.

Casa Italia • 2080 Constitution Blvd. • 924-1179
WHAT YOU CAN FIND THERE: A wide variety of hard to find ethnic items. Cheeses, deli, & more. Cooking classes. Prepared foods.

Geier's Sausage Kitchen • 7447 S. Tamiami Trl. • 923-3004
WHAT YOU CAN FIND THERE: Sausage & more sausage. Sarasota's best German market. Lots of smoked meats and deli items.

Karl Ehmer's Steakhouse • 4520 S. Tamiami Trl. • 922-3797
WHAT YOU CAN FIND THERE: Meat market. Skilled butchers, super helpful. Famous for Turducken. Also, full service restaurant.

M & M European Deli • 2805 Proctor Rd. • 922-1221
WHAT YOU CAN FIND THERE: European, Hungarian, & Polish grocery items. Great deli sandwiches. Borscht, goulash, & pierogis.

Morton's Gourmet Market • 1924 S. Osprey Ave. • 955-9856
WHAT YOU CAN FIND THERE: Upscale gourmet food items including a large selection of cheeses and wine. Great deli & carryout.

SARASOTA MARKETS AND SPECIALTY STORES

Morton's Siesta Market • 205 Canal Rd. • 349-1474
WHAT YOU CAN FIND THERE: Everyday grocery items plus a good selection of prepared foods for lunch and dinner. Cold beer.

Piccolo Italian Market • 6518 Gateway Ave. • 923-2202
WHAT YOU CAN FIND THERE: Italian market. Pastas, sauces, homebaked bread, and homemade Italian sausage. Sandwiches.

Southern Steer Butcher • 4084 Bee Ridge Rd. • 706-2625
WHAT YOU CAN FIND THERE: Big selection of pre-brined beef and chicken. Full butcher shop and lots of specialty items.

Walt's Fish Market • 4144 S. Tamiami Trl. • 921-4605
WHAT YOU CAN FIND THERE: Huge selection of fresh local fish & seafood. Stone crabs when in season. Smoked mullet spread!

MAIN STREET TRATTORIA
8131 Lakewood Main Street
941-907-1518
mstrattoria.com

LAKEWOOD RANCH	ITALIAN	COST: $$

HOURS: Mon-Thur, 4PM to 9PM • Fri, 4PM to 10PM
Sat, 12PM to 10PM • Sun, 12PM to 9PM

WHAT TO EXPECT: Great for a meet-up • Pizza • Good for families
Daily Happy Hour

CARRYOUT/DELIVERY INFO: Full menu is available for carryout. Curbside pick up. Delivery available through Bite Squad and Uber Eats.

SOME BASICS
Reservations:	YES
Spirits:	FULL BAR
Parking:	LOT/STREET
Outdoor Dining:	YES

SCAN FOR MENU

MAISON BLANCHE

2605 Gulf of Mexico Drive (Four Winds Beach Resort)
941-383-8088
themaisonblanche.com

LONGBOAT KEY	FRENCH	COST: $$$$

HOURS: Tues-Sun, 5:30PM to 9:30PM • CLOSED MONDAY

WHAT TO EXPECT: Date night! • Special occasions
Excellent service • Great wine list • Online reservations

CARRYOUT/DELIVERY INFO: Special changing menu for carryout and delivery. Curbside and contactless pick up available. Limited delivery is available through the restaurant.

SCAN FOR MENU

SOME BASICS

Reservations:	YES
Spirits:	BEER/WINE
Parking:	LOT
Outdoor Dining:	NO

MANDEVILLE BEER GARDEN

428 North Lemon Avenue
941-954-8688
mbgsrq.com

ROSEMARY DISTRICT	AMERICAN	COST: $$

HOURS: Mon & Tue, 4PM to 11PM • Wed & Thur, 11AM to 10PM
Fri & Sat, 11AM to 11PM • Sun, 11AM to 10PM

WHAT TO EXPECT: Beer & lots of it • Elevated brewpub fare
North downtown location • Just a cool place to hang out

CARRYOUT/DELIVERY INFO: Online ordering available. Full menu available for carryout. Delivery not available.

SCAN FOR MENU

SOME BASICS

Reservations:	NO
Spirits:	BEER/WINE
Parking:	LOT
Outdoor Dining:	YES

MAR-VISTA RESTAURANT
760 Broadway Street
941-383-2391
marvistadining.com

LONGBOAT KEY	AMERICAN	COST: $$

HOURS: Sun-Thur, 11:30AM to 9PM • Fri & Sat, 11:30AM to 10PM

WHAT TO EXPECT: Great for families • Big list of specialty drinks
Water view • Old Florida feel

CARRYOUT/DELIVERY INFO: Online ordering available. Full menu
available for carryout. Delivery not available.

SCAN FOR MENU

SOME BASICS
Reservations:	NO
Spirits:	FULL BAR
Parking:	LOT
Outdoor Dining:	YES

MARCELLO'S RISTORANTE
4155 South Tamiami Trail
941-921-6794
marcellosarasota.com

SOUTH TRAIL	ITALIAN	COST: $$$

HOURS: Mon-Sat, 5PM to 10PM
CLOSED SUNDAY

WHAT TO EXPECT: Nice wine list • Chef driven Italian cuisine
Intimate dining experience (10 tables)

CARRYOUT/DELIVERY INFO: Carryout and delivery not available.

SCAN FOR INFO

SOME BASICS
Reservations:	YES
Spirits:	BEER/WINE
Parking:	LOT
Outdoor Dining:	NO

MARINA JACK'S
2 Marina Plaza
941-365-4232
marinajacks.com

DOWNTOWN	SEAFOOD	COST: $$$

HOURS: Sun-Thur, 11AM to 9PM • Fri & Sat, 11AM to 10PM

WHAT TO EXPECT: Water view • Dinner cruises • Live music
Nice wine list • Live Music • Outdoor lounge

CARRYOUT/DELIVERY INFO: Carryout from patio only. Full patio menu available for carryout. Delivery not available.

SCAN FOR MENU

SOME BASICS
Reservations:	YES
Spirits:	FULL BAR
Parking:	VALET/LOT
Outdoor Dining:	YES

MATTISON'S CITY GRILLE
1 North Lemon Avenue
941-330-0440
mattisons.com

DOWNTOWN	AMERICAN	COST: $$

HOURS: Lunch - Daily, 11AM to 3PM
Dinner - Daily, 4:30PM to 10PM

WHAT TO EXPECT: Great for a date • Downtown meet-up spot
Live music • Great bar service • Happy Hour daily

CARRYOUT/DELIVERY INFO: Special limited menu available for carryout and delivery. Delivery available through Uber Eats, DoorDash and Bite Squad.

SCAN FOR MENU

SOME BASICS
Reservations:	YES
Spirits:	FULL BAR
Parking:	STREET
Outdoor Dining:	YES

MATTISON'S FORTY ONE
7275 South Tamiami Trail
941-921-3400
mattisons.com

SOUTH TRAIL	AMERICAN	COST: $$

HOURS: Mon-Thur, 11:30AM to 9PM • Fri, 11:30AM to 10PM
Sat, 4:30PM to 10PM • CLOSED SUNDAY

WHAT TO EXPECT: Large wine list • Brunch • Good value
Online reservations • Happy Hour menu

CARRYOUT/DELIVERY INFO: Full menu available for carryout.
Delivery available through DoorDash and Bite Squad.

SOME BASICS
SCAN FOR MENU

Reservations:	YES
Spirits:	FULL BAR
Parking:	LOT
Outdoor Dining:	NO

MEDITERRANEO
1970 Main Street
941-365-4122
mediterraneorest.com

DOWNTOWN	ITALIAN	COST: $$

HOURS: Lunch, Mon-Fri, 11:30AM to 2:30PM
Dinner, Daily from 5:30PM

WHAT TO EXPECT: Pizza • Good wine list • Italian specialties
Online reservations • Private party dining space

CARRYOUT/DELIVERY INFO: Online ordering available. Full menu
available for carryout and delivery. Curbside and contactless
pick up. Delivery through DoorDash.

SOME BASICS
SCAN FOR MENU

Reservations:	YES
Spirits:	FULL BAR
Parking:	STREET/GARAGE
Outdoor Dining:	YES

MELANGE

1568 Main Street
941-953-7111
melangesarasota.com

DOWNTOWN	AMERICAN	COST: $$$

HOURS: Lunch - Daily, 11:30AM to 2PM
Dinner - Daily, 5:30PM to 10PM

WHAT TO EXPECT: Great for a date • Adult dining experience
Open late night • Sophisticated menu options

CARRYOUT/DELIVERY INFO: Full menu is available for carryout
and delivery. Curbside and contactless pick up. Delivery available
through Bite Squad.

SCAN FOR MENU

SOME BASICS

Reservations:	YES
Spirits:	FULL BAR
Parking:	STREET
Outdoor Dining:	YES

MELLIE'S NEW YORK DELI

4650 FL 64
941-281-2139
melliesnewyorkdeli.com

BRADENTON	DELI	COST: $$

HOURS: Daily, 8AM to 5PM

WHAT TO EXPECT: Casual deli • NY deli food • 3 locations

CARRYOUT/DELIVERY INFO: Full menu available for carryout and
delivery. Delivery through Bite Squad, Uber Eats, GrubHub and
DoorDash.

SCAN FOR MENU

SOME BASICS

Reservations:	NONE
Spirits:	NONE
Parking:	LOT
Outdoor Dining:	NO

MI PUEBLO

8405 Tuttle Avenue*
941-359-9303
mipueblomexican.com

	MEXICAN	COST: $$

HOURS: Lunch & Dinner, Daily

WHAT TO EXPECT: Casual dining • Easy on the wallet
Catering available • Large menu of Mexican favorites

CARRYOUT/DELIVERY INFO: Online ordering available. Curbside
and contactless pick up available. Delivery not available.

SOME BASICS

SCAN FOR MENU

Reservations:	YES
Spirits:	FULL BAR
Parking:	LOT
Outdoor Dining:	NO

MICHAEL'S ON EAST

1212 East Avenue South
941-366-0007
bestfood.com

MIDTOWN PLAZA	AMERICAN	COST: $$$

HOURS: Tue-Sat, 5:30PM to 8:30PM
CLOSED SUNDAY AND MONDAY

WHAT TO EXPECT: Piano lounge • Catering • Fine dining
OpenTable reservations • AAA Four Diamond Award

CARRYOUT/DELIVERY INFO: Online ordering available.
Curbside and contactless pick up. Delivery available through the
restaurant.

SOME BASICS

SCAN FOR MENU

Reservations:	YES
Spirits:	FULL BAR
Parking:	VALET
Outdoor Dining:	YES

SALMON TARTARE

Chef de cuisine Johnny Zaki
1592 Wood Fired Kitchen & Cocktails

INGREDIENTS
18 oz. wild salmon fillet, boneless & skinless
2 avocados, cubed
4 tbsp olive oil
½ lime juice
1 whole lime zest
1 tbsp cilantro, chopped
1 tbsp chives, minced
½ tsp sriracha (adjust to taste)
1 tbsp Dijon mustard
2 tbsp mayonnaise

METHOD
In a small bowl, combine olive oil, lime juice, sriracha, Dijon mustard, mayonnaise, cilantro, and chives. Mix all ingredients together. Pour the marinade over diced salmon and avocado. Mix ingredients again. Using a stainless-steel round form centered on a plate, add salmon and avocado mixture. Sprinkle with chives and cilantro.

Serves 4

The modus operandi at 1592 is fire. The key feature – everything is cooked on wood fired grill. By creating intuitive culinary dishes with eclectic combinations of flavors, Executive Chef Alexandre Gosselin and Chef de Cuisine Johnny Zaki come together to orchestrate dishes that manipulate the flavors of local fresh ingredients, with a fine taste of modernity. 1592 is a great spot to indulge in comforting and flavorful cuisine, celebrate an occasion or simply sit at the bar and enjoy one of our signature cocktails.

MICHELLE'S BROWN BAG CAFÉ

1819 Main Street (City Center Building)
941-365-5858
michellesbrownbagcafe.com

DOWNTOWN	DELI	COST: $

HOURS: Mon-Fri, 7:30AM to 3PM
CLOSED SATURDAY & SUNDAY

WHAT TO EXPECT: Quick lunch • Easy on the wallet
Great meet-up spot • Super casual

CARRYOUT/DELIVERY INFO: Online ordering available. Full menu available for carryout and delivery. Delivery is available through the restaurant or Bite Squad.

SCAN FOR MENU

SOME BASICS

Reservations:	NO
Spirits:	BEER/WINE
Parking:	GARAGE/STREET
Outdoor Dining:	NO

MIGUEL'S

6631 Midnight Pass Road
941-349-4024
miguelsrestaurant.net

SIESTA KEY	FRENCH	COST: $$$

HOURS: Dinner, Daily from 5PM
Early Dinner Menu, 5PM to 6:30PM

WHAT TO EXPECT: Good wine list • Quiet atmosphere
Good early dining menu

CARRYOUT/DELIVERY INFO: Online ordering available. Full menu available for carryout. Delivery not available.

SCAN FOR MENU

SOME BASICS

Reservations:	YES
Spirits:	FULL BAR
Parking:	LOT
Outdoor Dining:	NO

MILLIES RESTAURANT

3900 Clark Road
941-923-4054
eatatmillies.com

AMERICAN	COST: $$

HOURS: Daily, 7AM to 2:30PM

WHAT TO EXPECT: Casual atmosphere • Good for families
Lots of parking

CARRYOUT/DELIVERY INFO: Online ordering available. Full menu available for carryout. You must call ahead for curbside pick up. Delivery not available.

SCAN FOR MENU

SOME BASICS

Reservations:	NO
Spirits:	NONE
Parking:	LOT
Outdoor Dining:	NO

MONK'S STEAMER BAR

6690 Superior Avenue
941-927-3388
monkssteamerbar.com

GULF GATE	SEAFOOD	COST: $$

HOURS: Mon-Thur, 3PM to 12AM • Fri & Sat, 12PM to 1AM
Sunday, 12PM to 12AM

WHAT TO EXPECT: Steamed everything! • Dive bar/great food
Locals favorite • Late night menu

CARRYOUT/DELIVERY INFO: Most menu items available for carryout. Delivery not available.

SCAN FOR MENU

SOME BASICS

Reservations:	NO
Spirits:	FULL BAR
Parking:	STREET/LOT
Outdoor Dining:	NO

MUNCHIES 420 CAFÉ
6639 Superior Avenue
941-929-9893
munchies420cafe.com

GULF GATE	AMERICAN	COST: $$

HOURS: Sun-Thur, 12PM to 3AM • Fri & Sat, 12PM to 4:20AM
Happy Hour, Daily, 12PM to 7PM

WHAT TO EXPECT: Crazy sandwiches! • Super laid back • Late night
Local favorite

CARRYOUT/DELIVERY INFO: Online ordering available. Full menu available for carryout and delivery. Delivery available through Bite Squad.

SOME BASICS
SCAN FOR MENU

Reservations:	NO
Spirits:	FULL BAR
Parking:	LOT
Outdoor Dining:	YES

---

99 BOTTLES TAPROOM
1445 Second Street
941-487-7874
99bottles.net

DOWNTOWN	BEER	COST: $$

HOURS: Mon-Thur, 3PM to 11PM
Fri - Sun, 9AM to 12AM

WHAT TO EXPECT: Big city feel • Knowledgeable bar staff
Small menu of good food • Great for an after work beer

CARRYOUT/DELIVERY INFO: Online ordering available. Full menu available for carryout. Curbside and contactless pick up. Delivery not available.

SOME BASICS
SCAN FOR MENU

Reservations:	NO
Spirits:	BEER/WINE
Parking:	STREET/GARAGE
Outdoor Dining:	NO

NANCY'S BAR-B-QUE

14475 State Road 70 E
941-999-2390
nancysbarbq.com

LWR	BBQ	COST: $

HOURS: Sun-Thur, 11AM to 8PM • Fri & Sat, 11AM to 9PM

WHAT TO EXPECT: Casual dining • Good for families
Catering available • Combo meals • Great pulled pork!

CARRYOUT/DELIVERY INFO: Online ordering available. Full menu available for carryout and delivery. Curbside and contactless pick up. Delivery available through Bite Squad and Grubhub.

SCAN FOR MENU

SOME BASICS

Reservations:	NO
Spirits:	FULLBAR
Parking:	LOT
Outdoor Dining:	YES

NAPULÈ RISTORANTE ITALIANO

7129 South Tamiami Trail
941-556-9639
napulesarasota.com

SOUTH TRAIL	ITALIAN	COST: $$$

HOURS: Mon-Thur, 11:30AM to 9:30PM
Fri & Sat, 11:30AM to 10:30PM • CLOSED SUNDAY

WHAT TO EXPECT: Upscale Italian dining • Great wood oven pizza
Very busy in season • Vibrant atmosphere

CARRYOUT/DELIVERY INFO: Full menu available for carryout and delivery. Curbside and contactless pick up. Delivery available through Bite Squad and DoorDash.

SCAN FOR MENU

SOME BASICS

Reservations:	YES
Spirits:	FULL BAR
Parking:	LOT
Outdoor Dining:	YES

NELLIE'S DELI
15 South Beneva Road
941-924-2705
nelliescatering.com

	DELI	COST: $$

HOURS: Mon-Fri, 7AM to 2:30PM • Sat, 8AM to 2:30PM
CLOSED SUNDAY

WHAT TO EXPECT: Deli & market • Great catering options
Casual dining • Good for families • Box lunches!

CARRYOUT/DELIVERY INFO: Full menu available for carryout and
delivery. Contactless pick up. Delivery available through
the restaurant.

SCAN FOR MENU

SOME BASICS
Reservations:	NO
Spirits:	NONE
Parking:	LOT
Outdoor Dining:	NO

NEW PASS GRILL & BAIT SHOP
1505 Ken Thompson Parkway
941-388-3050
newpassgrill.com

CITY ISLAND	AMERICAN	COST: $

HOURS: Daily, 8AM to 5PM

WHAT TO EXPECT: Casual dining • Water view • More than burgers
Bait & tackle shop

CARRYOUT/DELIVERY INFO: Full menu available for carryout.
Delivery not available.

SCAN FOR MENU

SOME BASICS
Reservations:	NO
Spirits:	BEER/WINE
Parking:	LOT
Outdoor Dining:	YES

SARASOTA
UPSCALE CHAIN DINING

Sarasota has a ton of great independently owned and operated restaurants. And, that's mostly what this dining book is all about. But, as with any decent size city, we've got our share of quality, upscale chain dining options, too.

We've taken the time to put together a list of some of our favorites. Just like the main section of the book, we didn't have the space to list them all. So, we curated a collection of the ones we think will give you a consistent and favorable dining experience.

We've tried to include a little bit of everything here for you. Some steakhouses, sushi, deli, and even pizza. You'll recognize most of the names I'm sure. There's something here for everyone.

Bonefish Grill • 3971 S. Tamiami Trl. • 924-9090
WHAT TO EXPECT: Upscale casual place to meetup with friends and enjoy drinks or dinner. Lots of seafood options. ($$)

Brio Tuscan Grille • 190 University Town Center Dr. • 702-9102
WHAT TO EXPECT: Italian cuisine. UTC. Online reservations. Lively atmosphere. Good for groups. ($$$)

California Pizza Kitchen • 192 N. Cattlemen Rd. • 203-6966
WHAT TO EXPECT: Pizzas & more. Good salads & pastas. Online ordering system. Catering. No reservations. ($$)

Capital Grille • 180 University Town Center Dr. • 256-3647
WHAT TO EXPECT: Big city steakhouse. Very upscale dining experience. Reservations/OpenTable. Private dining. ($$$$)

Chart House • 201 Gulf of Mexico Dr. • 383-5593
WHAT TO EXPECT: Fresh seafood. Nice gulf view. Always outstanding service. Classic upscale dining experience. ($$$)

Cheesecake Factory • 130 University Town Center Dr. • 256-3760
WHAT TO EXPECT: 200+ menu choices. Super large portions. Happy Hour. Catering. Very busy dining atmosphere. ($$$)

Fleming's Prime Steakhouse • 2001 Siesta Dr. • 358-9463
WHAT TO EXPECT: Super high quality steaks + service. Private dining. "Fleming's 100" wines. Happy Hour. ($$$$)

Hyde Park Steakhouse • 35 S. Lemon Ave. • 366-7788
WHAT TO EXPECT: Busy downtown location. Valet parking. Popular Happy Hour. "Early Nights" menu. Private dining. ($$$$)

Kona Grill • 150 University Town Center Dr. • 256-8050
WHAT TO EXPECT: Heavy Asian influence cuisine. Sushi. Lively dining experience. UTC Mall. Online reservations. ($$)

P.F. Changs Bistro • 766 S. Osprey Ave. • 296-6002
WHAT TO EXPECT: "Farm to Wok" Asian cuisine. Large menu. Busy, vibrant atmosphere. Good for groups. Online reservations. ($$$)

Rodizo Brazilian Steakhouse • 5911 Fruitville Rd. • 260-8445
WHAT TO EXPECT: Brazilian steakhouse experience. Rotisserie grilled meats. Table side service. Large gourmet salad bar. ($$$)

Ruth's Chris Steakhouse • 6700 S. Tamiami Trl. • 942-8982
WHAT TO EXPECT: Exceptional service. Older dining crowd. Large selection of USDA prime steaks. Great wine list. ($$$$)

Seasons 52 • 170 University Town Center Dr. • 702-5652
WHAT TO EXPECT: Seasonal menu selections. 52 wines by the glass. UTC Mall. Group dining options. Great service. ($$$)

Sophie's • 120 University Town Center Dr. • 444-3077
WHAT TO EXPECT: UTC inside Sak's 5th Avenue. "Ladies" lunch spot. Intimate dining experience. Great for private parties. ($$$)

OAK & STONE

5405 University Parkway*
941-225-4590
oakandstone.com

UPARK	AMERICAN	COST: $$

HOURS: Sun-Thur, 11AM to 10PM • Fri & Sat, 11AM to 12AM

WHAT TO EXPECT: Great for sports viewing • Lively atmosphere Live music • Large beer selection • Pizza too!

CARRYOUT/DELIVERY INFO: Online ordering. Full menu available for carryout & delivery. Curbside & contactless pick up. Delivery through Bite Squad, Grubhub, DoorDash and Uber Eats.

SCAN FOR MENU

SOME BASICS

Reservations:	NO
Spirits:	FULL BAR
Parking:	LOT
Outdoor Dining:	YES

OASIS CAFÉ

3542 South Osprey Avenue
941-957-1214
theoasiscafe.net

AMERICAN	COST: $$

HOURS: Mon-Fri, 7AM to 1:30PM • Sat & Sun, 8AM to 1:30PM

WHAT TO EXPECT: Breakfast & Lunch • Casual dining Very busy in season • Great bakery

CARRYOUT/DELIVERY INFO: Full menu available for carryout. Curbside and contactless pick up. Delivery not available.

SCAN FOR MENU

SOME BASICS

Reservations:	NO
Spirits:	BEER/WINE
Parking:	LOT
Outdoor Dining:	YES

OFF THE HOOK SEAFOOD COMPANY
6630 Gateway Avenue
941-923-5570
offthehooksrq.com

GULF GATE	SEAFOOD	COST: $$

HOURS: Daily, 11AM to 8PM

WHAT TO EXPECT: Great for casual seafood • Specialty martinis
Fish market • Seafood market

CARRYOUT/DELIVERY INFO: Online ordering available. Full menu available for carryout. Curbside pick up. Delivery not available.

SCAN FOR MENU

SOME BASICS
Reservations:	YES
Spirits:	FULL BAR
Parking:	LOT
Outdoor Dining:	NO

THE OLD SALTY DOG
5023 Ocean Boulevard*
941-349-0158
theoldsaltydog.com

SIESTA KEY	AMERICAN	COST: $$

HOURS: Sun-Thur, 11AM to 9:30PM • Fri & Sat, 11AM to 10PM

WHAT TO EXPECT: Locals love it • Vacation feel • Cold beer
Busy during season • Siesta Village • Friendly bar staff

CARRYOUT/DELIVERY INFO: Online ordering available. Full menu available for carryout. Delivery not available.

SCAN FOR MENU

SOME BASICS
Reservations:	NO
Spirits:	FULL BAR
Parking:	STREET
Outdoor Dining:	YES

New England Style Lobster Roll

Chef John Hentschl - Daiquiri Deck

INGREDIENTS
2 lb pre-cooked Maine lobster meat, drained
2 cups of celery (diced ¼")
3 tsp fresh dill herb
1½ tsp Old Bay
1½ tsp garlic powder
1½ tsp onion powder
2 cups of mayonnaise
8 King's Hawaiian Hot Dog Rolls

METHOD
Mix together, Old Bay, garlic powder, and onion powder. Set aside. Put all the lobster meat, celery, dill into a big mixing bowl. Mix lightly. Add the mayonnaise and spice mix.
Mix thoroughly.
Serve on a toasted Hawaiian Hot Dog Roll.

Serves 8

Looking for a cool way to start or end your day? The Daiquiri Deck has you covered. They're known for their large selection of unique, signature frozen daiquiris and casual beach cuisine. With restaurants located in Siesta Village, South Siesta Key, St. Amands Circle, Island of Venice, and Anna Maria Island, you'll never be far from great food and a great time. For more information on all of their locations, find them on the web at, daiquirideck.com.

O'LEARY'S TIKI BAR & GRILL

5 Bayfront Drive
941-953-7505
olearystikibar.com

DOWNTOWN	AMERICAN	COST: $$

HOURS: Sun-Thur, 8AM to 10PM • Fri & Sat, 8AM to 11PM

WHAT TO EXPECT: Live music • Beach bar • Cold beer
Great views • Watersports rentals

CARRYOUT/DELIVERY INFO: Full menu available for carryout. No phone-in ordering. Must order carryout at the restaurant. Delivery not available.

SOME BASICS

SCAN FOR MENU

Reservations:	NO
Spirits:	FULL BAR
Parking:	LOT
Outdoor Dining:	YES

OPHELIA'S ON THE BAY

9105 Midnight Pass Road
941-349-2212
opheliasonthebay.net

SIESTA KEY	AMERICAN	COST: $$$

HOURS: Dinner Nightly, 5PM to 10PM

WHAT TO EXPECT: Great for a date • Nice water view
Good wine list • OpenTable reservations

CARRYOUT/DELIVERY INFO: Full menu available for carryout. Curbside pick up. Delivery not available.

SOME BASICS

SCAN FOR MENU

Reservations:	YES
Spirits:	FULL BAR
Parking:	VALET
Outdoor Dining:	YES

ORIGIN CRAFT BEER & PIZZA CAFÉ

1837 Hillview Street*
941-316-9222
originpizzacafe.com

SOUTHSIDE VILLAGE	PIZZA	COST: $$

HOURS: Sun-Thur, 11AM to 1AM • Fri & Sat, 11AM to 2AM

WHAT TO EXPECT: Neighborhood feel • Open late • Friendly staff
Local favorite • New (2020) 2nd location • Craft beer

CARRYOUT/DELIVERY INFO: Full menu available for carryout
and delivery. Curbside and contactless pick up. Delivery available
through Bite Squad, Uber Eats and Grubhub.

SCAN FOR MENU

SOME BASICS

Reservations:	NO
Spirits:	BEER/WINE
Parking:	LOT/STREET
Outdoor Dining:	YES

ORTYGIA

1418 13th Street West
941-741-8646
ortygiarestaurant.com

BRADENTON	SICILIAN	COST: $$

HOURS: Lunch, Thur-Sat, 12PM to 2PM
Dinner, Tues-Sat, 5PM to 9PM • CLOSED SUNDAY

WHAT TO EXPECT: Eclectic cuisine • Village of the Arts
Online reservations

CARRYOUT/DELIVERY INFO: A special carryout menu is
available. Curbside pick up under special circumstances.
Delivery available through the restaurant.

SCAN FOR MENU

SOME BASICS

Reservations:	YES
Spirits:	BEER/WINE
Parking:	STREET
Outdoor Dining:	YES

THE OVERTON

1420 Boulevard of the Arts
941-552-6927
theovertonsrq.com

ROSEMARY DISTRICT	AMERICAN	COST: $$

HOURS: Tue-Sun, 8AM to 7PM
CLOSED MONDAY

WHAT TO EXPECT: Super casual • Good for a meet-up
Specialty coffee

CARRYOUT/DELIVERY INFO: Full menu available for carryout.
Delivery not available.

SOME BASICS

SCAN FOR INFO

Reservations:	NONE
Spirits:	BEER/WINE
Parking:	STREET/LOT
Outdoor Dining:	YES

OWEN'S FISH CAMP

516 Burns Court
941-951-6936
owensfishcamp.com

BURNS COURT	SEAFOOD	COST: $$

HOURS: Daily, 4PM to 9PM

WHAT TO EXPECT: Fun dining experience • Good for families
Busy in season • Parking can be a challenge

CARRYOUT/DELIVERY INFO: Carryout on a limited basis. No
curbside or contactless pick up options. Call ahead to restaurant
to see if carryout is available. Delivery not available.

SOME BASICS

SCAN FOR MENU

Reservations:	NO
Spirits:	FULL BAR
Parking:	STREET/LOT
Outdoor Dining:	YES

PACIFIC RIM

1859 Hillview Street
941-330-8071
pacrimsrq.com

SOUTHSIDE VILLAGE	ASIAN	COST: $$

HOURS: Mon-Fri, 11:30AM to 2PM • Mon-Thur, 5PM to 9:30PM
Fri & Sat, 5PM to 10:30PM • Sun, 5PM to 9PM

WHAT TO EXPECT: Fun dining experience • Sushi & more
Parking usually available • Happy Hour

CARRYOUT/DELIVERY INFO: Full menu available for carryout and delivery. Curbside pick up. Delivery through Bite Squad.

SCAN FOR MENU

SOME BASICS

Reservations:	4 OR MORE
Spirits:	FULL BAR
Parking:	LOT/STREET
Outdoor Dining:	YES

THE PARROT PATIO BAR & GRILL

3602 Webber Street
941-952-3352
theparrotpatiobar.com

	AMERICAN	COST: $$

HOURS: Mon-Thur, 11AM to 11PM • Fri & Sat, 11AM to 12AM
Happy Hour, Mon-Fri, 11:30 to 7PM

WHAT TO EXPECT: Very casual • Sports bar feel • LIVE music
NFL football package • Good for groups

CARRYOUT/DELIVERY INFO: Online ordering available. Full menu available for carryout. Curbside pick up. Delivery not available.

SCAN FOR MENU

SOME BASICS

Reservations:	NO
Spirits:	FULL BAR
Parking:	LOT
Outdoor Dining:	YES

PASCONE'S RISTORANTE
5239 University Parkway
941-210-7368
pascones.com

LAKEWOOD RANCH	ITALIAN	COST: $$$

HOURS: Tues-Thur, 4:30PM to 8:30PM • Fri & Sat, 4:30PM to 9PM
Sun, 10AM to 2PM & 4:30PM to 8:30PM• CLOSED MONDAY

WHAT TO EXPECT: Lively feel • Happy Hour daily • Kids menu
Lots of parking • Good for groups

CARRYOUT/DELIVERY INFO: Online ordering. Full menu available
for carryout. Curbside and contactless pick up.
Delivery not available.

SCAN FOR MENU

SOME BASICS
Reservations:	YES
Spirits:	FULL BAR
Parking:	LOT
Outdoor Dining:	NO

PASTRY ART
1512 Main Street
941-955-7545
pastryartbakerycafe.com

DOWNTOWN	AMERICAN	COST: $$

HOURS: Mon-Thur, 7AM to 7PM • Fri & Sat, 7AM to 10PM
Sun, 8AM to 5PM

WHAT TO EXPECT: Great for a coffee date • Live music
Wi-Fi • Busy weekend spot

CARRYOUT/DELIVERY INFO: Full menu available for carryout
and delivery. Delivery available until 2PM. Delivery is through the
restaurant.

SCAN FOR MENU

SOME BASICS
Reservations:	NO
Spirits:	BEER/WINE
Parking:	STREET
Outdoor Dining:	YES

PATRICK'S 1481

1481 Main Street
941-955-1481
patricks1481.com

DOWNTOWN	AMERICAN	COST: $$

HOURS: Sun, 11:30AM to 9PM • Mon, 11:30AM to 10PM
Tue-Thur, 11:30AM to 9PM • Fri & Sat, 11:30AM to 10PM

WHAT TO EXPECT: Sat. & Sun. brunch • Local favorite
Good Happy Hour

CARRYOUT/DELIVERY INFO: Online ordering available. Full menu
available for carryout and delivery. Delivery available
through DoorDash.

SCAN FOR MENU

SOME BASICS

Reservations:	5 OR MORE
Spirits:	FULL BAR
Parking:	STREET/VALET
Outdoor Dining:	YES

PAZZO SOUTHSIDE

1936 Hillview Street
941-260-8831
pazzosouthside.com

SOUTHSIDE VILLAGE	ITALIAN	COST: $$

HOURS: Mon-Thur, 11AM to 9PM • Fri, 11AM to 10PM
Sat, 5PM to 10PM • CLOSED SUNDAY

WHAT TO EXPECT: Good for a date • Pizza
Bar for solo diners • New location (2020)

CARRYOUT/DELIVERY INFO: Online ordering available. Special
carryout menu. Curbside and contactless pick up.
Delivery not available.

SCAN FOR MENU

SOME BASICS

Reservations:	YES
Spirits:	BEER/WINE
Parking:	LOT/STREET
Outdoor Dining:	YES

Food Trucks are popular. And, just like every other great food community, we've got our share roaming the streets. Here's a little basic info to help you navigate through the maze of local mobile dining options. These are a few of our favorites!

MOUTHOLE BBQ
What They Serve: BBQ, BBQ, AND BBQ. Beef, pork, ribs, and chicken. Also some great desserts.
Where You Can Find Them: Various locations around the Sarasota area. Check their Facebook page for details.
Info at: moutholebbq.com

THE AMISH BAKING COMPANY
What They Serve: Giant, homemade, and delicious donuts and pretzels. A big line for a reason!
Where You Can Find Them:
Phillippi Farmhouse Market. Oct-Apr, 8AM to 2PM.
Info at: Amish Baking Company Facebook Page

MOBSTAH LOBSTAH
What They Serve: "Seafood to die for!" Serving up Maine lobster rolls and a whole lot more.
Where You Can Find Them:
Calusa Brewing, various area seafood events.
Info at: www.mobstahlobstah.com or FB Page

HAMLET'S EATERY
What They Serve: Tacos and slider boxes. Both meat and vegan options are available.
Where You Can Find Them:
The Bazaar on Apricot & Lime
Info at: hamletseatery.com

For more info on these and other Sarasota area food trucks visit SRQFoodtruckAlliance.com.

PHILLPPI CREEK OYSTER BAR

5353 South Tamiami Trail
941-925-4444
creekseafood.com

SOUTH TRAIL	SEAFOOD	COST: $$

HOURS: Sun-Thur, 11AM to 9PM • Fri & Sat, 11AM to 9PM

WHAT TO EXPECT: Great for families • Water view • Casual dining
Busy during season • Good for kids

CARRYOUT/DELIVERY INFO: Full menu available for carryout.
Curbside pick up. Delivery not available.

SCAN FOR MENU

SOME BASICS
Reservations:	NO
Spirits:	FULL BAR
Parking:	LOT
Outdoor Dining:	YES

PHO CALI

1578 Main Street
941-955-2683
phocalisarasota.com

DOWNTOWN	VIETNAMESE	COST: $

HOURS: Mon-Thur, 11AM to 9PM • Fri & Sat, 11AM to 9:30PM
CLOSED SUNDAY

WHAT TO EXPECT: Great service • Casual dining
Easy on the wallet • Good for families • Noodle bowls!

CARRYOUT/DELIVERY INFO: Full menu available for carryout.
Delivery not available.

SCAN FOR MENU

SOME BASICS
Reservations:	NO
Spirits:	BEER/WINE
Parking:	STREET
Outdoor Dining:	NO

PICCOLO ITALIAN MARKET & DELI

6518 Gateway Avenue
941-923-2202
piccolomarket.com

GULF GATE	ITALIAN	COST: $

HOURS: Tue-Fri, 10AM to 6PM • Sat, 10AM to 4PM
CLOSED SUNDAY

WHAT TO EXPECT: Great for a quick lunch • Italian market
Super casual • Easy on the wallet • Catering available

CARRYOUT/DELIVERY INFO: Online ordering available. Full menu available for carryout and delivery. Curbside and contactless pick up. Delivery through DoorDash.

SCAN FOR MENU

SOME BASICS

Reservations:	NO
Spirits:	NONE
Parking:	LOT
Outdoor Dining:	NO

PIER 22

1200 1st Avenue West
941-748-8087
pier22dining.com

BRADENTON	SEAFOOD	COST: $$$

HOURS: Mon-Thur, 11:30AM to 10PM • Fri, 11:30AM to 10:30PM
Sat, 8AM to 10:30PM • Sun, 8AM to 10PM

WHAT TO EXPECT: Great for a date • Water view • Good wine list
OpenTable reservations • Weekend brunch

CARRYOUT/DELIVERY INFO: Online ordering available. Full menu available for carryout. Curbside and contactless pick up. Delivery not available.

SCAN FOR MENU

SOME BASICS

Reservations:	YES
Spirits:	FULL BAR
Parking:	LOT
Outdoor Dining:	YES

THE POINT

131 Bayview Drive
941-786-3890
eviesonline.com/location/the-point

OSPREY	SEAFOOD	COST: $$

HOURS: Daily, 11AM to 10PM

WHAT TO EXPECT: Three floors of dining • Great gulf views
Good for groups and parties • Arrive by boat!

CARRYOUT/DELIVERY INFO: Full menu available for carryout.
Delivery not available.

SCAN FOR MENU

SOME BASICS

Reservations:	YES
Spirits:	FULL BAR
Parking:	LOT
Outdoor Dining:	YES

POP'S SUNSET GRILL

112 Circuit Road (ICW Marker 10 by boat)
941-488-3177
popssunsetgrill.com

NOKOMIS	SEAFOOD	COST: $$

HOURS: Daily, 11AM to 10PM

WHAT TO EXPECT: Drive thru "Pontiki" food & bev pickup for boats
Water view • Vacation atmosphere • Great for families

CARRYOUT/DELIVERY INFO: Most menu items available
for carryout and delivery. Curbside and dockside pick up.
Contactless pick up. Delivery through DoorDash.

SCAN FOR MENU

SOME BASICS

Reservations:	YES
Spirits:	FULL BAR
Parking:	LOT
Outdoor Dining:	YES

PUB 32
8383 South Tamiami Trail
941-952-3070
pub32sarasota.com

SOUTH TRAIL	IRISH	COST: $$

HOURS: Tue-Sun, 12PM to 9PM • CLOSED MONDAY

WHAT TO EXPECT: Great casual dining • Good beer list
Live music • Monday night whiskey club

CARRYOUT/DELIVERY INFO: Full menu available for carryout and delivery. Curbside pick up. Delivery available through Bite Squad.

SCAN FOR MENU

SOME BASICS

Reservations:	YES
Spirits:	FULL BAR
Parking:	LOT
Outdoor Dining:	YES

RASOI INDIAN KITCHEN

NEW

7119 South Tamiami Trail
941-921-9200
rasoisarasota.com

SOUTH TRAIL	INDIAN	COST: $$

HOURS: Lunch, Tue-Fri, 11AM to 3PM • Sat & Sun, 11AM to 3:30PM
Dinner, Tue-Sun , 5PM to 10PM • CLOSED MONDAY

WHAT TO EXPECT: Upscale, but, casual dining • Lots of parking
Authentic Indian Cuisine

CARRYOUT/DELIVERY INFO: Full menu available for carryout and delivery. Curbside pick up. Delivery available through Bite Squad, Uber Eats, DoorDash and Grubhub.

SCAN FOR MENU

SOME BASICS

Reservations:	YES
Spirits:	BEER/WINE
Parking:	LOT
Outdoor Dining:	NO

Crab Cakes with Bay Scallop Succotash

Chef Robby Clark, Blasé Southern Style

INGREDIENTS
1 lb crab meat
½ cup dried bread crumbs
1 cup mayonnaise
¼ cup scallion, finely chopped
1 large egg
1 tbsp Old Bay seasoning
1 tsp mustard powder
½ tsp Worcestershire Sauce
¼ tsp hot sauce
peanut or vegetable oil
1 lemon

METHOD
In large bowl mix together mayonnaise, scallion, egg, Old Bay, mustard powder, Worcestershire, and hot sauce. Fold in the bread crumbs and crab meat. Form into patties, about 6-8 oz each. Heat oil in flat frying pan on med/high heat until sizzling. Sear crab cakes about 3-5 min on each side. Blot on paper towel when done and serve on their own with lemon wedges and the sauce of your choosing or on top of Bay Scallop Succotash.

BAY SCALLOP SUCCOTASH

INGREDIENTS
10 oz frozen lima beans, thawed
10 oz frozen corn kernels, thawed
1 lb bay scallops
3 tbsp butter
2 tbsp roasted garlic puree
½ cup onions, chopped

½ cup grape tomatoes, sliced in half
1 tsp paprika
1 tsp dried Italian herbs
1 tsp garlic powder
1 tsp onion powder
Salt & pepper to taste
½ cup chicken stock
¼ cup white wine

METHOD

Saute scallops. Add lima beans, corn, and onions. Cook until onions are translucent. Deglaze pan with white wine. Add roasted garlic puree and tomatoes. Simmer for a few minutes, to cook off the wine a bit. Add chicken stock and cook until reduced by half. Fold in butter and spices.

Serves 3

Blasé Southern Style, located in Southside Village neighborhood. For more info visit www.blasehillview.com or call 941-312-6850.

REEF CAKES

NEW

1812 South Osprey Avenue
941-444-7968
reefcakes.com

SOUTHSIDE VILLAGE	SEAFOOD	COST: $$

HOURS: Daily, Lunch & Dinner

WHAT TO EXPECT: Fish Cakes • Casual dining experience

CARRYOUT/DELIVERY INFO: Full menu available for carryout. Curbside and contactless pick up available. Delivery available through DoorDash, Uber Eats and Bite Squad.

SOME BASICS

Reservations:	NO
Spirits:	BEER/WINE
Parking:	STREET
Outdoor Dining:	NO

SCAN FOR INFO

RENDEZ-VOUS FRENCH BAKERY

5336 Clark Road*
941-924-1234
rendezvoussarasota.com

FRENCH	COST: $$

HOURS: Tues-Sat, 7:30AM to 3PM • Sun, 8AM to 3PM
CLOSED MONDAY

WHAT TO EXPECT: Fresh French baked goods • Catering
Fantastic French omelets! • Very casual

CARRYOUT/DELIVERY INFO: Full menu available for carryout.
Curbside pick up. Delivery not available.

SCAN FOR MENU

SOME BASICS

Reservations:	NO
Spirits:	NONE
Parking:	LOT
Outdoor Dining:	NO

REYNA'S TAQUERIA

935 North Beneva Road (Sarasota Commons)
941-260-8343
reynastaqueria.com

SARASOTA COMMONS	MEXICAN	COST: $

HOURS: Sun-Thur, 11AM to 8PM • Fri & Sat, 11AM to 10PM

WHAT TO EXPECT: Family friendly • Super easy on the wallet
Lots of parking • Authentic Mexican cuisine

CARRYOUT/DELIVERY INFO: Full menu available for carryout
and delivery. Curbside and contactless pick up. Delivery available
through Bite Squad and Uber Eats.

SCAN FOR MENU

SOME BASICS

Reservations:	NO
Spirits:	BEER/WINE
Parking:	LOT
Outdoor Dining:	NO

RICK'S FRENCH BISTRO

2177 Siesta Drive
941-957-0533
ricksfrenchbistro.com

SOUTHGATE	FRENCH	COST: $$$

HOURS: Tues-Sat, 5PM to 10PM
CLOSED SUNDAY & MONDAY

WHAT TO EXPECT: Quiet dining experience • Authentic French
Small, but nice wine list

CARRYOUT/DELIVERY INFO: Full menu available for carryout.
Curbside pick up. Delivery not available.

SCAN FOR MENU

SOME BASICS

Reservations:	YES
Spirits:	BEER/WINE
Parking:	LOT
Outdoor Dining:	NO

RICO'S PIZZERIA

1902 Bay Road
941-366-8988
ricospizzapie.com

	ITALIAN	COST: $$

HOURS: Sun-Thur & Sat, 11AM to 10PM • Fri, 11AM to 11PM

WHAT TO EXPECT: Family pizza place • Italian specialty dishes
Sandwiches • Casual dining experience

CARRYOUT/DELIVERY INFO: Online ordering. Full menu available
for carryout and delivery. Curbside and contactless pick up.
Delivery available through restaurant.

SCAN FOR MENU

SOME BASICS

Reservations:	NO
Spirits:	BEER/WINE
Parking:	LOT
Outdoor Dining:	NO

Stuffed Chicken with Poblano Cream Sauce

Chef Greg Campbell, GROVE Restaurant

INGREDIENTS
6 oz chicken breast
Breadcrumbs, as needed
1 whole egg
4 oz buttermilk

STUFFING
2 oz cream cheese
1 oz bacon
1 tsp basil
1 tsp rosemary
1 tsp oregano

METHOD
Lay chicken on cutting board between 2 sheets of plastic wrap. Pound with mallet until approximately 1/8 of an inch thick. Mix stuffing ingredients together. Place in a neat pile in the center of the chicken breast. Roll the chicken so stuffing is not exposed.
Mix egg and buttermilk together. Use as bath for the chicken. When you remove the chicken from the bath roll the chicken through the breadcrumbs until chicken is completely covered. Pan sear chicken 4 minutes on each side. Place in oven at 350 degrees for 7-8 minutes and temp to 165 degrees.

POBLANO CREAM SAUCE
INGREDIENTS
6 roasted poblano peppers, stemmed and seeded
2 fresh poblano peppers, stemmed and seeded

6 jalapeno peppers stemmed and seeded
8 garlic cloves
2 qts heavy cream
Salt and pepper to taste

METHOD
Place all ingredients in a large sauce pot. Cook over
medium heat for 20 minutes or until sauce begins to
thicken. Puree until smooth and strain through chinios.
When chicken is ready, plate and top with poblano cream
sauce.

Serves 1

*GROVE specializes in contemporary American offerings and on-
site event planning. The menu is elevated yet approachable and
locally inspired. Overlooking the charming Main Street center,
at GROVE there's room for everyone at the table! We serve
breakfast, brunch, lunch and dinner and offer direct delivery to
the LWR area. More info at: GroveLWR.com or 941-893-4321.*

ROESSLER'S
2033 Vamo Way
941-966-5688
roesslersrestaurant.com

SOUTH TRAIL	EUROPEAN	COST: $$$

HOURS: Dinner, Tues-Sun, 5PM to close
CLOSED MONDAY

WHAT TO EXPECT: Good wine list • Private dining room
Family owned & operated since 1978 • Online reservations

CARRYOUT/DELIVERY INFO: Full menu available for carryout.
Curbside pick up. Delivery not available.

SCAN FOR MENU

SOME BASICS
Reservations:	YES
Spirits:	FULL BAR
Parking:	LOT
Outdoor Dining:	YES

Craft beer, brew pubs, and full on local breweries. Sarasota is not immune from the small batch beer craze. As a matter of fact, we've got some damn good beer craftsmen right here in town. Oh, and along with these local artisans are some great places to down a few unique brews. Here's a list of some of our local favorites. - Cheers!

SARASOTA BREWERIES & BREWPUBS

BIG TOP BREWING
6111 Porter Way
Sarasota, FL 34232
941-371-2939
bigtopbrewing.com

CALUSA BREWING
5701 Derek Avenue
Sarasota, FL 34233
941-922-8150
calusabrewing.com

DARWIN BREWING COMPANY
803 7th Avenue W
Bradenton, FL 34205
941-747-1970
darwinbrewingco.com

JDUB'S BREWING COMPANY
1215 Mango Avenue
Sarasota, FL 34237
941-955-2739
jdubsbrewing.com

MOTORWORKS BREWING
1014 9th Street W
Bradenton, FL 34205
941-567-6218
motorworksbrewing.com

SARASOTA BREWING COMPANY
6607 Gateway Avenue
Sarasota, FL 34231
941-925-2337
sarasotabrewing.com

SARASOTA BEER BARS

MANDEVILLE BEER GARDEN
428 N. Lemon Avenue
Sarasota, FL 34236
941-954-8688
mandevillebeergarden.com

99 BOTTLES
1445 2nd Street
Sarasota, FL 34236
941-487-7874
99bottles.net

SHAMROCK PUB
2257 Ringling Boulevard
Sarasota, FL 34237
941-952-1730
www.shamrocksarasota.com

ROSEBUD'S STEAKHOUSE & SEAFOOD

2215 South Tamiami Trail
941-918-8771
rosebudssarasota.com

OSPREY	STEAKHOUSE	COST: $$$

HOURS: Tues-Sun, 4PM to 10PM
CLOSED MONDAY

WHAT TO EXPECT: Early bird dining • Private dining room
Aged, hand cut, Angus steaks • Established 1995

CARRYOUT/DELIVERY INFO: Online ordering. Full menu available for carryout. Curbside and contactless pick up.
Delivery not available.

SCAN FOR MENU

SOME BASICS

Reservations:	YES
Spirits:	FULL BAR
Parking:	LOT
Outdoor Dining:	NO

THE ROSEMARY

411 North Orange Avenue
941-955-7600
therosemarysarasota.com

ROSEMARY DISTRICT	AMERICAN	COST: $$

HOURS: Daily, 8AM to 2PM

WHAT TO EXPECT: Casual dining • Busy in season
Downtown, north of Fruitville • Nice lunch spot

CARRYOUT/DELIVERY INFO: Full menu available for carryout.
Please call the restaurant for delivery options.

SCAN FOR MENU

SOME BASICS

Reservations:	YES
Spirits:	BEER/WINE
Parking:	STREET
Outdoor Dining:	YES

ROSEMARY AND THYME

511 North Orange Avenue
941-955-7600
therosemarysarasota.com

ROSEMARY DISTRICT	AMERICAN	COST: $$$

HOURS: Wed-Sat 4:30PM to 9PM

WHAT TO EXPECT: Upscale, but, casual • OpenTable reservations
Great appetizers • Don't forget dessert

CARRYOUT/DELIVERY INFO: Special three-course carryout
menu available. Full menu also available for carryout.
Delivery not available.

SOME BASICS

SCAN FOR INFO

Reservations:	YES
Spirits:	FULL BAR
Parking:	STREET
Outdoor Dining:	NO

SAGE

1216 First Street
941-445-5660
sagesrq.com

DOWNTOWN	AMERICAN	COST: $$$

HOURS: Tues-Thur, 5PM to 10PM
Fri & Sat, 5PM to 11PM

WHAT TO EXPECT: Upscale dining • Private event space
OpenTable reservations • Rooftop is great for a date

CARRYOUT/DELIVERY INFO: Full menu available for carryout.
Curbside pick up. Delivery not available.

SOME BASICS

SCAN FOR MENU

Reservations:	YES
Spirits:	FULL BAR
Parking:	LOT/STREET
Outdoor Dining:	YES

THE SANDBAR

100 Spring Avenue
941-778-0444
sandbardining.com

ANNA MARIA	AMERICAN	COST: $$

HOURS: Mon-Thur, 11:30AM to 9PM • Fri & Sat, 11:30AM to 10PM
Sun, 10AM to 9PM

WHAT TO EXPECT: Great causal beach dining • Island feel
Good for a private beach party

CARRYOUT/DELIVERY INFO: Online ordering available. Full menu
available for carryout. Delivery not available.

SCAN FOR MENU

SOME BASICS
Reservations:	NO
Spirits:	FULL BAR
Parking:	LOT
Outdoor Dining:	YES

SARASOTA BREWING COMPANY

6607 Gateway Avenue
941-925-2337
sarasotabrewing.com

GULF GATE	AMERICAN	COST: $$

HOURS: Sun-Thur, 11AM to 12PM • Fri & Sat, 11AM to 1AM

WHAT TO EXPECT: Craft brewpub • Established 1989
Chicago style pizza & beef sandwiches • Good for sports

CARRYOUT/DELIVERY INFO: Full menu available for carryout
and delivery. Curbside and contactless pick up. Delivery available
through Bite Squad.

SCAN FOR MENU

SOME BASICS
Reservations:	YES
Spirits:	BEER/WINE
Parking:	LOT
Outdoor Dining:	NO

SARDINIA

5770 South Tamiami Trail
941-702-8582
sardiniasrq.com

SOUTH TRAIL	ITALIAN	COST: $$$

HOURS: Mon-Sat, 5PM to 10PM
CLOSED SUNDAY

WHAT TO EXPECT: Small & intimate dining • Homemade dishes
Private dining room available • Chef driven menu

CARRYOUT/DELIVERY INFO: Full menu available for carryout.
30% off carryout bottles of wine. Delivery available
through DoorDash.

SCAN FOR MENU

SOME BASICS

Reservations:	YES
Spirits:	BEER/WINE
Parking:	LOT
Outdoor Dining:	NO

SCHNITZEL KITCHEN

6521 Superior Avenue
941-922-9299
schnitzelkitchen.com

GULF GATE	GERMAN	COST: $$

HOURS: Tues-Sat, 4PM to 9PM
CLOSED SUNDAY & MONDAY

WHAT TO EXPECT: Casual ethnic cuisine • Homemade dishes
BIG German beer selection

CARRYOUT/DELIVERY INFO: Full menu available for carryout and
delivery. Curbside pick up. Delivery available through Bite Squad
and DoorDash.

SCAN FOR MENU

SOME BASICS

Reservations:	YES
Spirits:	BEER & WINE
Parking:	LOT/STREET
Outdoor Dining:	NO

SCREAMING GOAT TAQUERIA

6606 Superior Avenue
941-210-3992
screaming-goat.com

GULF GATE	MEXICAN	COST: $

HOURS: Mon-Sat, 11AM to 8PM • CLOSED SUNDAY

WHAT TO EXPECT: Super casual • Taco shack • Family friendly
Great for a quick lunch or dinner

CARRYOUT/DELIVERY INFO: Online ordering available. Full menu available for carryout and delivery. Delivery available through Uber Eats.

SCAN FOR MENU

SOME BASICS

Reservations:	NONE
Spirits:	BEER/WINE
Parking:	LOT/STREET
Outdoor Dining:	NO

SEABAR

`NEW`

6540 Superior Avenue
941-923-6605
seabarsrq.com

GULF GATE	ASIAN	COST: $$

HOURS: Sun-Thur, 4PM to 12AM • Fri & Sat, 4PM to 2AM

WHAT TO EXPECT: Pan Asian cuisine • Local seafood focus
Casual dining experience.

CARRYOUT/DELIVERY INFO: Full menu is available for carryout. Delivery not available.

SCAN FOR MENU

SOME BASICS

Reservations:	NO
Spirits:	FULL BAR
Parking:	LOT/STREET
Outdoor Dining:	NO

SELVA GRILL

1345 Main Street*
941-362-4427
selvagrill.com

DOWNTOWN	PERUVIAN	COST: $$$

HOURS: Mon-Thur, 5PM to 11PM • Fri & Sat, 5PM to 1PM

WHAT TO EXPECT: Great for a date • Main & Palm
OpenTable reservations

CARRYOUT/DELIVERY INFO: Full menu available for carryout.
Curbside pick up not available. Delivery not available.

SOME BASICS

Reservations:	YES
Spirits:	FULL BAR
Parking:	STREET/PALM GARAGE
Outdoor Dining:	YES

SCAN FOR MENU

SHAKESPEARE'S ENGLISH PUB

3550 South Osprey Avenue
941-364-5938
shakespearesenglishpub.com

	BRITISH	COST: $$

HOURS: Daily, 11:30AM to 9PM

WHAT TO EXPECT: Great for after work meet-up • Good for lunch
Fantastic burger • Traditional English fare

CARRYOUT/DELIVERY INFO: Full menu available for carryout and
delivery. Curbside pick up. Delivery available through Grubhub,
Bite Squad and DoorDash.

SOME BASICS

Reservations:	NO
Spirits:	BEER/WINE
Parking:	LOT
Outdoor Dining:	YES

SCAN FOR MENU

YOUR BEER DRINKING STYLE GUIDE

Ed Paulsen, Calusa Brewing

"What are you in the mood for?" It's my first and favorite question when greeting a customer at Calusa Brewing. Step up to a bar or glance at a shelf these days and you're bound to notice the astonishing variety of beers, both in brands and styles. This wide range of flavors and characters beg us to ask of ourselves: "What type of experience do I want? What flavors am I craving? Do I want something buoyant or thought-provoking, full and smooth, or clean and brisk?" As the late British writer Michael Jackson wrote, what is the "perfect beer for the perfect moment?"

With the aim of satisfying your thirst and curiosity, I would like to present this selected list of beer styles including suggestions for some excellent local and classic examples to look out for.

Abbey Ale

Most associated with the Belgian monastic brewing traditions, there are some fine US examples, as well. Expect medium-to-high strength and effervescence with notes of spice and dark fruits. These beers pair well with food and are appropriately worthy of contemplation. *Examples: St. Bernardus, Leffe. See: Trappist, Dubbel, Tripel*

Berliner Weisse

Berlin's famous wheat beer, traditionally served with an herb or fruit syrup on the side. Light, sparkling with an appetizing tartness, it is a popular base style for playful American interpretations. *Examples: Bell's Oarsman Ale, Big Top Ringmaster Raspberry*

Bock

Originating in the mid-north of Einbeck in Lower Saxony, Bocks are the famed rich, strong lagers of Bavaria. Often associated with spring (Amber-colored Maibock) or Lent (Doppel (double) bock). American versions such as Shiner Bock, Genessee Bock, Anheuser-Busch Amberbock, tend to be modest, amber Lagers. *Examples: Ayinger Celebrator, Paulaner Salvator*

Brown Ale

Associated with light-bodied ales from the north of England. American examples may be full of flavor; malty, lightly roasty, or chocolaty, and even have a pronounced hop character in aroma and/or finish. *Examples: Cigar City Maduro, Newcastle Brown Ale*

Dubbel

A deep mahogany Belgian abbey-style ale usually around 7% ABV. Very expressive of dark fruits and spice on account of unique yeast strains.
Examples: Westmalle Dubbel, Chimay Red, Ommegang Abbey Ale.

Gose

Pronounced 'GO-zuh,' a German wheat beer of low to mid-strength with a refreshing tartness and interestingly spiced with coriander seed and salt. Another playful canvas for American brewers to experiment with and flattering for certain types of fruit additions.
Examples: Anderson Valley Gose, Dogfish Seaquench

Hefeweizen
Originally a beer enjoyed only by Bavarian royalty, Hefeweizen is the famous cloudy wheat beer traditionally served in a tall glass with a grand foam.
Examples: Franziskaner, Erdinger, Paulaner, Widmer, Sierra Nevada Kellerweis. See: Wheat Beer

Imperial Stout
Strongest of the stout family historically produced in England for export to the Russian court in the 18th century. It is roasty, full, and even bracingly bitter in some American examples. A strong candidate for barrel aging and often a welcome playground for dessert-like additions (vanilla, chocolate).
Examples: Sierra Nevada Narwhal, Cigar City Marshal Zhukov, Victory Storm King, North Coast Old Rasputin.

International Lager
Perhaps the world's best-selling beer - a derivative of the original Pilsner from 1842. As the style gained fame and traveled, it tended to become more streamlined and has lost some character. *Examples: Heineken, Tsing Tao, Kingfisher, Kronenberg, Stella Artois.*

IPA
Originating in the UK, this style has come to embody American craft beer more than any other. Enthusiastic and occasionally unapologetic celebration of the flavors and aromas of the wonderful hop. Modern American versions may be explosively aromatic with notes of citrus, pine, and even tropical fruits. The 'hazy' American style that originated in the Northeast US within the last decade features a softer mouthfeel and sense of 'juiciness'
Examples: Cigar City Jai Alai, Calusa Zote and Citronious, Stone IPA, Bells Two-Hearted, Founders All Day IPA, Big Top Ashley Gang.

Kolsch

The famous beer of Cologne (Köln) is traditionally served in thin, narrow glasses called Stange (rod). Straw gold with a light, refreshing character and slight fruitiness from a cool-fermenting ale strain unique to the style. American versions often have more hop character in either aroma or bitterness (or both). *Examples: JDubs Poolside, Gaffel.*

Lager

Not a style but a type of fermentation and family of beers associated with Germany, Denmark and what is now the Czech Republic. *Examples include: Pilsner, Oktoberfest, Bock, Vienna Lager, Schwarzbier and others.*

Lambic

Perhaps the most unique beers in the world, Lambics are a true taste of terroir and a unique window into the past. Produced in a small area in and around Brussels they eschew traditional fermentation and brewers yeast by harnessing wild yeast and cultures unique to this area. Long aging in oak vessels produce beers of astonishing tartness and earthy minerality. Traditionally, fruits such as cherry, or recently raspberry, are added which can complement the tart, dry character.

Light Beer

Much like International Lager, yet even more distant from the Bohemian original golden beer, Pilsner. Driven by branding, they are produced primarily for mass consumption or calorie reduction and tend to lack any discernible character of malt, hops, or fermentation.

Marzen/Oktoberfest

A moderately strong, malt-accented lager associated with the fall season and Oktoberfest celebration (Munich). Traditionally German but popular with American craft brewers. *Examples: Samuel Adams, Hofbrau, Ayinger, Weihenstephaner.*

Pale Ale

A balanced British style of mid-strength with lean toward hop character. American examples, personified by Sierra Nevada, often have even more hop aroma and flavor with more neutral malt and fermentation character.
Examples: Sierra Nevada, Fuller's London Pride, Oskar Blues Dale's Pale Ale

Pilsner

The world's first golden lager born in Pilsen/Plzen in Bohemia in 1842. Dry, aromatic, and appetizing with a classic herbal, floral hop character and crisp finish, Pilsner is one of the world's classic beer styles.
Examples: Pilsner Urquell, Victory Prima Pils, Green Bench Postcard Pils, Calusa Outbound and Dry-Hopped Pils, Darwin Pirata Pils.

Porter

The predecessor and twin to stout and the root of every dark beer. Once one of the world's most popular styles, it flourished in the 18th century as British industry, seafaring, and imperialism spread it throughout the world. Nearly extinct in its home country, as recently as the 1970s, it was revived by American brewers. Today, it is a roasty, chocolatey beer of mid-strength. *Examples: Founders Porter, Fuller's London Porter, Bell's Porter, Sierra Nevada Porter, Deschutes Black Butte.*

Saison

Typically a golden Belgian Ale with a pronounced fruit/spice character, a noticeable hop character and quenching dryness. Historically an enigma, in a modern sense, nearly anything Belgian-esqe that brewers do not want to weigh down with a label. May be oak-aged or oak-fermented with wild yeasts presenting fruity, slightly tart character. *Examples, Saison Dupont, Boulevard Tank 7, Jolly Pumpkin Bam Biere and Oro de Calabaza, Fantome, Goose Island Sophie.*

Stout

Dark ales of English origin with a focus on the chocolatey, coffee-like character of roasted grains. A true family of beers ranging from the light, dry character of Guinness through the regal intensity of Russian Imperial Stout. Includes styles like Oatmeal Stout (addition of oats), Milk/ Sweet Stout, Foreign/Tropical stouts. Dry and appetizing, Irish Dry Stout is exemplified by Guinness with the crisp, bright character of roasted barley.
Examples: Left Hand Milk Stout, Deschutes Obsidian Stout, Sierra Nevada Stout, Guinness, Lion Stout.

Trappist

Not a style per se but a designation of production and origin relating to the Trappist Monasteries. Popularly associated with Belgium in brands such as Chimay, most produce a range of Abbey-style ales (Dubbel, Tripel, etc). *Examples: Chimay, Rochefort, Orval, Westmalle.*

Triple/Tripel

A strong, golden ale of around 9% originating with the Westmalle Abbey in Belgium. Many fine craft examples abound, including Victory Brewing's Golden Monkey.
Examples: Westmalle Tripel, Chimay White, Victory Golden Monkey See: Abbey Ale, Trappist

Wheat Beer

A family of ales containing a portion of wheat in addition to barley, traditionally ranging from the western coast of Belgium and the Netherlands through Germany and Poland. Generally golden and occasionally gently spiced, they all share a drinkable lively carbonation. US examples, such as Bell's Oberon, often lack the spice and fruit character of German or Belgian versions. See: Hefeweizen, Gose, Berliner Weisse, Witbier/White Ale

Witbier

An ancient Dutch/Flemish style of wheat beer with an expressive yeast strain, and creamy, soft drinkability. Traditionally spiced with coriander seed and orange peel. *Examples: Hoegaarden, Allagash White, Blue Moon, Big Top Trapeze Monk.* See: Wheat Beer

Founded in 2016, Calusa Brewing is a family-owned and operated craft brewery in Sarasota, Florida. Production specializes in fresh, hop-forward beers along with a barrel-aged program for mixed fermentation and clean beers We want to welcome you to visit our 8,500 square foot brewing facility and tasting room located in South Sarasota.

SHANER'S PIZZA

6500 Superior Avenue
941-927-2708
shanerspizza.com

GULF GATE	PIZZA	COST: $$

HOURS: Sun & Mon, 11:30AM to 9PM • Tue-Sat, 4:30PM to 10PM

WHAT TO EXPECT: Pizza and more • Casual atmosphere
Good place to catch the game

CARRYOUT/DELIVERY INFO: Full menu available for carryout and delivery, Curbside pick up. Delivery available through Bite Squad.

SCAN FOR MENU

SOME BASICS
Reservations:	NO
Spirits:	BEER/WINE
Parking:	LOT/STREET
Outdoor Dining:	YES

SHARKEY'S ON THE PIER

1600 Harbor Drive South
941-488-1456
sharkysonthepier.com

VENICE	AMERICAN	COST: $$

HOURS: Sun-Thur, 11:30AM to 10PM • Fri & Sat, 11:30AM to 11PM

WHAT TO EXPECT: Live music • On the beach • Very "Florida"
Voted Florida's Best Beach Bar ('13, '18, '19)

CARRYOUT/DELIVERY INFO: Full menu available for carryout.
Curbside and contactless pick up. Delivery not available.

SOME BASICS

SCAN FOR MENU

Reservations: YES
Spirits: FULL BAR
Parking: LOT
Outdoor Dining: YES

SHORE DINER

465 John Ringling Boulevard*
941-296-0301
dineshore.com

ST. ARMANDS	AMERICAN	COST: $$$

HOURS: Mon-Sat, 12PM to 9PM • Sun, 10AM to 9PM

WHAT TO EXPECT: Online reservations • Busy during season
Good wine list • Happy Hour

CARRYOUT/DELIVERY INFO: Online ordering available. Full menu
available for carryout. Curbside and contactless pick up.
Delivery not available.

SOME BASICS

SCAN FOR MENU

Reservations: YES
Spirits: FULL BAR
Parking: STREET
Outdoor Dining: YES

SARASOTA SUSHI
YOUR BEST ROLLS ROLL HERE!

Looking for sushi in Sarasota? You're going to have a decision to make. We have some fantastic and creative sushi chefs that call Sarasota their home. We've got 20+ places where you can indulge. Space is limited here, so we have personally curated a list of some of the best places in town (subject to debate of course). Whether, you're sitting at the bar or at a table with a group of friends you can't go wrong with any of these places. Oh, just say "OMAKASE" and watch the magic happen...

DaRuMa Japanese Steak House • 5459 Fruitville Rd • 342-6600
WHAT TO EXPECT: Sushi + Teppan tableside cooking. This place is great for groups and big parties. Now open in The Landings.

Drunken Poet Cafe • 1572 Main St. • 955-8404
WHAT TO EXPECT: Sushi + Thai. A large selection of sushi. Downtown location. Also, lots of cooked options to choose from.

Jpan Restaurant • 3800 S. Tamiami Trl. • 954-5726
WHAT TO EXPECT: Always great. Never a miss here. BIG sushi menu. Super creative presentations. Also, across from UTC mall.

Kiyoshi's Sushi • 6550 Gateway Ave. • 924-3781
WHAT TO EXPECT: Nigiri, sashimi, and maki. That's pretty much it. This is a sushi restaurant. Very upscale creations & presentations.

Pacific Rim • 1859 Hillview St. • 330-0218
WHAT TO EXPECT: One of Sarasota's most established sushi restaurants. Good for groups. Lots of cooked dishes too.

Star Thai & Sushi • 240 Avenida Madera • 217-6758
WHAT TO EXPECT: Really creative & well presented sushi dishes. Lots of Thai choices as well. Friendly Siesta Key atmosphere.

Yume Sushi • 1537 Main St. • 363-0604
WHAT TO EXPECT: Downtown's go-to sushi place. Lots & lots of sushi. Also, a big assortment of other options. Great bar, too!

SIEGFRIED'S RESTAURANT

1869 Fruitville Road
941-330-9330
siegfrieds-restaurant.com

DOWNTOWN	GERMAN	COST: $$

HOURS: Wed-Sun, 4PM to 10PM
CLOSED MONDAY & TUESDAY

WHAT TO EXPECT: Casual dining • Family owned
Authentic German cuisine • German beer-garden

CARRYOUT/DELIVERY INFO: Full menu available for carryout.
Curbside pick up. Delivery not available.

SOME BASICS

SCAN FOR MENU

Reservations:	YES
Spirits:	BEER/WINE
Parking:	LOT/STREET
Outdoor Dining:	YES

SIESTA KEY OYSTER BAR (SKOB)

5238 Ocean Boulevard
941-346-5443
skob.com

SIESTA KEY	AMERICAN	COST: $$

HOURS: Mon-Thur, 11AM to 12AM • Fri & Sat, 11AM to 2AM
Sun, 9AM to 12AM

WHAT TO EXPECT: Vacation atmosphere • Live music daily
Sunday brunch • Great for families • Busy in season

CARRYOUT/DELIVERY INFO: Most menu items available for
carryout. Curbside pick up. Delivery not available.

SOME BASICS

SCAN FOR MENU

Reservations:	NO
Spirits:	FULL BAR
Parking:	LOT/STREET
Outdoor Dining:	YES

SIMON'S COFFEE HOUSE
5900 South Tamiami Trail
941-926-7151
simonstogo.com

SOUTH TRAIL	DELI	COST: $$

HOURS: Mon-Sat, 8AM to 4PM

WHAT TO EXPECT: Sandwiches • Salads • Vegan & Vegetarian options

CARRYOUT/DELIVERY INFO: Full menu available for carryout and delivery. Curbside and contactless pick up. Delivery available through Bite Squad, Uber Eats and DoorDash.

SCAN FOR MENU

SOME BASICS

Reservations:	NO
Spirits:	BEER/WINE
Parking:	LOT
Outdoor Dining:	NO

SMOQEHOUSE

NEW

6112 South Tamiami Trail
941-923-9090
smoqehouse.com

SOUTH TRAIL	BBQ	COST: $$

HOURS: Mon-Sat, 11AM to 8PM • CLOSED SUNDAY

WHAT TO EXPECT: BBQ • Great sandwiches • Super casual
Good for a quick lunch

CARRYOUT/DELIVERY INFO: Online ordering available. Full menu available for carryout and delivery. Delivery is available through Bite Squad.

SCAN FOR MENU

SOME BASICS

Reservations:	NO
Spirits:	BEER/WINE
Parking:	LOT
Outdoor Dining:	NO

SNOOK HAVEN

5000 East Venice Avenue
941-485-7221
snookhaven.com

VENICE	AMERICAN	COST: $$

HOURS: Wed-Sun, 11:30AM to 8PM
CLOSED MONDAY & TUESDAY

WHAT TO EXPECT: Old Florida • Super unique setting
Canoe & kayak rentals • Banjo Thursdays!

CARRYOUT/DELIVERY INFO: Full menu available for carryout.
Curbside and contactless pick up. Delivery not available.

SOME BASICS

SCAN FOR MENU

Reservations:	NO
Spirits:	BEER/WINE
Parking:	LOT
Outdoor Dining:	YES

SOUTH PHILLY CHEESESTEAKS

NEW

1439 Main Street*
941-330-8208
thecheapestwaytophilly.com/mainstreet

DOWNTOWN	AMERICAN	COST: $$

HOURS: Mon-Sat, 10:30AM to 9PM • CLOSED SUNDAY

WHAT TO EXPECT: Cheesesteaks! • Shakes and malts
Great for a quick lunch • Authentic Philly hoagies

CARRYOUT/DELIVERY INFO: Full menu available for carryout and
delivery. Delivery available through Bite Squad and Uber Eats.

SOME BASICS

SCAN FOR MENU

Reservations:	NO
Spirits:	BEER/WINE
Parking:	STREET
Outdoor Dining:	NO

SOUTHSIDE DELI

1825 Hillview Street
941-330-9302
southsidedelisarasota.com

SOUTHSIDE VILLAGE	DELI	COST: $$

HOURS: Mon-Fri, 7AM to 8PM • Sat, 7AM to 6PM
CLOSED SUNDAY

WHAT TO EXPECT: Deli sandwiches • Quick service
Great salads • Drive thru service

CARRYOUT/DELIVERY INFO: Full menu available for carryout
and delivery. Drive through pick up. Delivery available through
Grubhub.

SCAN FOR MENU

SOME BASICS

Reservations:	NO
Spirits:	NONE
Parking:	STREET
Outdoor Dining:	YES

SPEAKS CLAM BAR

29 North Boulevard of Presidents*
941-232-7633
speaksclambar.com

ST. ARMANDS	SEAFOOD	COST: $$$

HOURS: Mon-Wed, 4:30M to 10PM • Thur, 11AM to 10PM
Fri & Sat, 11AM to11PM • Sun, 12PM to 10PM

WHAT TO EXPECT: Clams! • "Italian" clam bar • Online reservations
Gluten free menu • Good for groups

CARRYOUT/DELIVERY INFO: Online ordering available. Full menu
available for carryout and delivery. Curbside and contactless
pick up. Delivery available through Uber Eats and Bite Squad.

SCAN FOR MENU

SOME BASICS

Reservations:	YES
Spirits:	FULL BAR
Parking:	GARAGE/STREET
Outdoor Dining:	YES

SPEARFISH GRILLE

1265 Old Stickney Point Road
941-349-1971
spearfishgrille.com

SIESTA KEY	SEAFOOD	COST: $$

HOURS: Daily, 11AM to 10PM

WHAT TO EXPECT: Super casual • Island feel
Small menu • Good for families

CARRYOUT/DELIVERY INFO: Full menu available for carryout.
Delivery not available.

SCAN FOR MENU

SOME BASICS
Reservations:	NONE
Spirits:	FULL BAR
Parking:	LOT/STREET
Outdoor Dining:	YES

SPICE STATION

1438 Boulevard of the Arts
941-343-2894
spicestationsrq.com

DOWNTOWN	THAI/SUSHI	COST: $$

HOURS: Mon-Thur, 11AM to 9PM • Fri, 11AM to 9:30PM
Sat 12PM to 9:30PM • CLOSED SUNDAY

WHAT TO EXPECT: Casual Asian cuisine • Quaint and comfortable
Vegetarian options • Thai and sushi

CARRYOUT/DELIVERY INFO: Full menu available for carryout and
delivery. Curbside pick up. Delivery available through Bite Squad,
Uber Eats and DoorDash.

SCAN FOR MENU

SOME BASICS
Reservations:	YES
Spirits:	BEER/WINE
Parking:	LOT/STREET
Outdoor Dining:	NO

STAR THAI AND SUSHI

240 Avenida Madera*
941-217-6758
starthaisushisiestakey.com

SIESTA KEY	ASIAN	COST: $$

HOURS: Wed-Mon, 12PM to 11PM • CLOSED TUESDAY

WHAT TO EXPECT: Sushi • Siesta Village • Very friendly staff
Live music

CARRYOUT/DELIVERY INFO: Full menu available for carryout and
delivery. Delivery through Bite Squad, Uber Eats and DoorDash.

SCAN FOR MENU

SOME BASICS

Reservations:	YES
Spirits:	FULL BAR
Parking:	STREET/LOT
Outdoor Dining:	NO

STATE STREET EATING HOUSE

1533 State Street
941-951-1533
statestreetsrq.com

DOWNTOWN	AMERICAN	COST: $$

HOURS: Lunch: Tues-Sat, 11:30AM to 2PM
Dinner: Tues-Sat, 5:30PM to 9:30PM

WHAT TO EXPECT: Great for a date • Comfort food • Good wine list
Sat. & Sun. brunch

CARRYOUT/DELIVERY INFO: Online ordering available. Full menu
available for carryout and delivery. Curbside pick up. Delivery
available through Bite Squad.

SCAN FOR MENU

SOME BASICS

Reservations:	5 OR MORE
Spirits:	FULL BAR
Parking:	LOT
Outdoor Dining:	YES

STATION 400
400 Lemon Avenue*
941-906-1400
station400.com

ROSEMARY DISTRICT	AMERICAN	COST: $$

HOURS: Daily, 7:30AM to 2:30PM

WHAT TO EXPECT: Great for lunch meet-up • Lots of pancakes
Soups, salads, & sandwiches • Catering

CARRYOUT/DELIVERY INFO: Full menu available for carryout.
Delivery not available.

SCAN FOR MENU

SOME BASICS
Reservations:	NO
Spirits:	BEER/WINE
Parking:	LOT
Outdoor Dining:	YES

STOTTLEMEYER'S SMOKEHOUSE
19 East Road
941-312-5969
stottlemyerssmokehouse.com

	BBQ	COST: $$

HOURS: Mon-Wed, 11:30AM to 8PM • Thur, 11:30AM to 9PM
Fri & Sat, 11:30PM to 10PM • Sun, 11:30AM to 9PM

WHAT TO EXPECT: Good for families • Easy on the wallet
Live music • Casual Florida dining experience

CARRYOUT/DELIVERY INFO: Online ordering available. Full menu
available for carryout and delivery. Curbside pick up. Delivery
available through Chow Now.

SCAN FOR MENU

SOME BASICS
Reservations:	YES
Spirits:	FULL BAR
Parking:	LOT
Outdoor Dining:	YES

SUMMER HOUSE STEAK & SEAFOOD

149 Avenida Messina
941-260-2675
summerhousesiestakey.com

SIESTA KEY	STEAKHOUSE	COST: $$$

HOURS: Sun-Thur, 4PM to 10PM
Fri & Sat, 4PM to 11PM

WHAT TO EXPECT: Bustling atmosphere • Happy Hour
Convenient Siesta Key location • Excellent wine list

CARRYOUT/DELIVERY INFO: Full menu available for carryout.
Curbside pick up available by special request only.
Delivery not available.

SCAN FOR MENU

SOME BASICS

Reservations:	YES
Spirits:	FULL BAR
Parking:	STREET/VALET
Outdoor Dining:	NO

SUN GARDEN CAFÉ

210 Avenida Madera
941-346-7170
sungardencafe.com

SIESTA KEY	AMERICAN	COST: $$

HOURS: Daily, 7:30AM to 1:30PM

WHAT TO EXPECT: Casual island lunch • Nice outdoor seating
Sandwich/soup/salad combos

CARRYOUT/DELIVERY INFO: Full menu available for carryout.
Curbside pick up. Delivery not available.

SCAN FOR MENU

SOME BASICS

Reservations:	NO
Spirits:	BEER/WINE
Parking:	STREET
Outdoor Dining:	YES

SUNNYSIDE CAFÉ

4900 North Tamiami Trail
941-359-9500
sunnysidecafesrq.com

NORTH TRAIL	AMERICAN	COST: $$

HOURS: Mon-Fri, 9AM to 3PM • Sat, 8AM to 3PM
Dinner: Tues-Sat, 5PM to 9PM

WHAT TO EXPECT: Pet friendly • Vegan options • Casual dining
House cured lox

CARRYOUT/DELIVERY INFO: Full menu available for carryout and delivery. Delivery through Bite Squad.

SCAN FOR MENU

SOME BASICS
Reservations:	NO
Spirits:	BEER/WINE
Parking:	LOT
Outdoor Dining:	YES

TAMIAMI TAP

711 South Osprey Avenue
941-500-3182
tamiamitap.com

DOWNTOWN	AMERICAN	COST: $$

HOURS: Tues-Fri, 4PM to 12AM • Sat, 5PM to 12AM
Sun, 11AM to 9PM • CLOSED MONDAY

WHAT TO EXPECT: Sat. & Sun. Brunch • Good Happy Hour
Live music • Late night

CARRYOUT/DELIVERY INFO: Online ordering available. Full menu available for carryout and delivery. Delivery available through DoorDash and Bite Squad.

SCAN FOR MENU

SOME BASICS
Reservations:	NO
Spirits:	FULL BAR
Parking:	LOT
Outdoor Dining:	YES

TANDOOR

8453 Cooper Creek Boulevard
941-926-3077
tandoorsarasota.net

UPARK	INDIAN	COST: $$

HOURS: Lunch, Tue-Sun, 11:30AM to 2:30PM • CLOSED MONDAY
Dinner, Sun-Thur, 5PM to 9:30PM • Fri & Sat, 5PM to 10PM

WHAT TO EXPECT: Great for groups • Tandoor cooking
Authentic Indian cuisine • Catering available

CARRYOUT/DELIVERY INFO: Full menu available for carryout and delivery. Delivery through DoorDash, Uber Eats, Bite Squad and Grubhub.

SCAN FOR MENU

SOME BASICS

Reservations:	YES
Spirits:	BEER/WINE
Parking:	LOT
Outdoor Dining:	NO

TASTE OF ASIA

4413 South Tamiami Trail
941-923-2742
tasteofasiasarasota.com

SOUTH TRAIL	ASIAN	COST: $$

HOURS: Tue-Thur, 3PM to 8PM • Fri - Sun, 11:30AM to 8:30PM
CLOSED MONDAY

WHAT TO EXPECT: Good for groups • Family owned
Lots of parking • Gluten free options • Great Thai & Laotian

CARRYOUT/DELIVERY INFO: Full menu available for carryout.
Curbside pick up. Delivery not available.

SCAN FOR MENU

SOME BASICS

Reservations:	YES
Spirits:	FULL BAR
Parking:	LOT
Outdoor Dining:	YES

TASTY HOME COOKIN'

3854 South Tuttle Avenue
941-921-4969
tastyhomecookinsarasota.com

TUTTLE BEE PLAZA	AMERICAN	COST: $

HOURS: Mon-Fri, 7AM to 6PM • Sat, 7AM to 2PM
Sun, 8AM to 2PM

WHAT TO EXPECT: Great for families • Easy on the wallet
Comfort food • Casual dining • Good for kids

CARRYOUT/DELIVERY INFO: Full menu available for carryout and delivery. Delivery available through Bite Squad.

SCAN FOR MENU

SOME BASICS

Reservations:	NO
Spirits:	BEER/WINE
Parking:	LOT
Outdoor Dining:	NO

TOASTED MANGO CAFÉ

430 North Tamiami Trail*
941-388-7728
toastedmangocafe.com

NORTH TRAIL	AMERICAN	COST: $$

HOURS: Daily, 7AM to 3PM

WHAT TO EXPECT: Good for families • Casual dining • Great service
Lots of menu choices

CARRYOUT/DELIVERY INFO: Full menu available for carryout. Curbside pick up. Limited delivery available. Call the restaurant to order and for delivery details.

SOME BASICS

Reservations:	NO
Spirits:	FULL BAR
Parking:	LOT
Outdoor Dining:	NO

SCAN FOR MENU

TOMMY BAHAMA CAFÉ

300 John Ringling Boulevard
941-388-2888
tommybahama.com

ST. ARMANDS	AMERICAN	COST: $$

HOURS: Sun-Thur, 11AM to 8:30PM • Fri & Sat, 11AM to 9:30PM

WHAT TO EXPECT: Great for a relaxing lunch • Island time Happy Hour
St. Armands Circle • OpenTable reservations

CARRYOUT/DELIVERY INFO: Online ordering. Full menu available
for carryout and delivery. Curbside and contactless pick up.
Delivery available through Chow Now.

SCAN FOR MENU

SOME BASICS
Reservations:	YES
Spirits:	FULL BAR
Parking:	STREET
Outdoor Dining:	YES

TONY'S CHICAGO BEEF

6569 Superior Avenue*
941-922-7979
tonyschicagobeef.com

GULF GATE	AMERICAN	COST: $

HOURS: Mon-Sat, 11AM to 9PM
CLOSED SUNDAY

WHAT TO EXPECT: Great for lunch • Easy on the wallet
Chicago style food • Counter and table seating

CARRYOUT/DELIVERY INFO: Full menu available for carryout and
delivery. Delivery available through Bite Squad.

SCAN FOR MENU

SOME BASICS
Reservations:	NO
Spirits:	BEER/WINE
Parking:	LOT/STREET
Outdoor Dining:	YES

TURTLES ON LITTLE SARASOTA BAY

8875 Midnight Pass Road
941-346-2207
turtlesrestaurant.com

SIESTA KEY	AMERICAN	COST: $$

HOURS: Daily, 11:30AM to 9PM

WHAT TO EXPECT: Right on the water • Old style Florida dining
Sunday brunch • Happy Hour specials

CARRYOUT/DELIVERY INFO: Special carryout menu. Curbside
and contactless pick up. Delivery not available.

SCAN FOR MENU

SOME BASICS

Reservations:	YES
Spirits:	FULL BAR
Parking:	LOT
Outdoor Dining:	YES

EXPERIENCE A SARASOTA FOOD TOUR

KEY CULINARY TOURS

WHAT TO EXPECT: Culinary tours of St. Armands Circle and
downtown Sarasota. They also offer "Happy Place" tours. A great
opportunity to sample some delicious local food and maybe
make a new friend or three. Fun for a group for sure.
MORE INFO: keyculinarytours.com or 941-893-4664

TASTE MAGAZINE PROGRESSIVE DINNERS

WHAT TO EXPECT: Remember the neighborhood progressive
dinner? This your chance to experience an upgraded version
of the classic food adventure. Taste Magazine sponsors
themed progressive dinners about once every six weeks
starting December 11th. The walking historical and food tour of
Bradenton departs every Wednesday & Thursday at 1PM. That's
a fun way to spend a Florida afternoon.
MORE INFO: tasteweb.net or 941-366-7950

THE MAKING OF A CLASSIC CHICAGO FAVORITE!

Tony's Chicago Beef is located in the Gulf Gate neighborhood.
Serving a menu of Chicago favorites including beef sandwiches,
Chicago dogs and more. More info at tonyschicagobeef.com.

Illustration by South Haven, Michigan artist, Jennifer Sistrunk.
To see more of her work visit: jennifersistrunk.com

VALENTINO'S PIZZERIA
4045 Clark Road*
941-921-9600
valentinopizzeria.com

	PIZZA	**COST: $$**

HOURS: Mon-Thur, 11AM to 9PM
Fri & Sat, 11AM to 10PM • Sun, 4PM to 9PM

WHAT TO EXPECT: Good for groups • Private events & catering
Good for families • Lots of parking

CARRYOUT/DELIVERY INFO: Full menu available for carryout and
delivery. Curbside pick up. Delivery available through Bite Squad.

SCAN FOR MENU

SOME BASICS
Reservations:	YES
Spirits:	BEER/WINE
Parking:	LOT
Outdoor Dining:	NO

VEG
6538 Gateway Avenue
941-312-6424
vegsrq.com

GULF GATE	**VEGETARIAN**	**COST: $$**

HOURS: Lunch, Mon-Sat, 11AM to 2PM
Dinner, Mon-Sat, 5PM to 8PM • CLOSED SUNDAY

WHAT TO EXPECT: Vegan/Veg • Daily specials
One of Sarasota's oldest vegetarian restaurants

CARRYOUT/DELIVERY INFO: Online ordering. Full menu available
for carryout and delivery. Curbside pick up. Delivery through Bite
Squad and Uber Eats.

SCAN FOR MENU

SOME BASICS
Reservations:	YES
Spirits:	BEER/WINE
Parking:	LOT/STREET
Outdoor Dining:	NO

VENEZIA

373 St. Armands Circle
941-388-1400
venezia-1966.com

ST ARMANDS	ITALIAN	COST: $$

HOURS: Daily, 11AM to 10PM

WHAT TO EXPECT: Great for a date • Pizza
Vibrant atmosphere • Busy during season/weekends

CARRYOUT/DELIVERY INFO: Online ordering. Full menu available for carryout. Curbside pick up. Delivery not available.

SCAN FOR MENU

SOME BASICS

Reservations:	YES
Spirits:	FULL BAR
Parking:	STREET
Outdoor Dining:	YES

VERONICA FISH & OYSTER

1830 South Osprey Avenue
941-366-1342
veronicafishandoyster.com

SOUTHSIDE VILLAGE	SEAFOOD	COST: $$$

HOURS: Tue-Thur, 5PM to 9PM • Fri & Sat, 5PM to 10PM
CLOSED SUNDAY & MONDAY

WHAT TO EXPECT: Busy, lively dining room • Handmade cocktails
Raw bar • Upscale dining

CARRYOUT/DELIVERY INFO: ** *At press time, we were not able to verify the carryout and delivery options for this restaurant. We suggest you call for their most up to date information.* **

SCAN FOR MENU

SOME BASICS

Reservations:	YES
Spirits:	FULL BAR
Parking:	LOT/STREET
Outdoor Dining:	YES

VIENTO KITCHEN + BAR

4711 Gulf of Mexico Drive (Zota Beach Resort)
941-248-1211
zotabeachresort.com/dining/viento-kitchen

LONGBOAT KEY	AMERICAN	COST: $$$

HOURS: Daily, Breakfast, Lunch, & Dinner

WHAT TO EXPECT: Nice wine list • Good for groups
Spectacular Gulf views

CARRYOUT/DELIVERY INFO: Full menu available for carryout.
Carryout available for resort guests only.

SCAN FOR MENU

SOME BASICS

Reservations:	YES
Spirits:	FULL BAR
Parking:	VALET
Outdoor Dining:	YES

ABOUT US

Way back in April 2002 we started dineSarasota as a way to bring up to date restaurant and dining information to Sarasota locals and visitors. Our annual printed dining guides and our website, dineSarasota.com, have grown right along with the ever expanding Sarasota dining scene. Whether you're just visiting or you're a native, we're here to help you make the most of your local dining experiences.

VILLAGE CAFÉ

5133 Ocean Boulevard
941-349-2822
villagecafeonsiesta.com

SIESTA KEY	AMERICAN	COST: $$

HOURS: Daily, 7AM to 2:30PM

WHAT TO EXPECT: Family owned • Dog friendly outdoor dining
Casual dining • Heart of Siesta Village • Good for familes

CARRYOUT/DELIVERY INFO: Full menu available for carryout and
delivery. Curbside pick up. Delivery available through Bite Squad
and Uber Eats.

SCAN FOR MENU

SOME BASICS

Reservations:	NO
Spirits:	BEER/WINE
Parking:	STREET
Outdoor Dining:	YES

WALT'S FISH MARKET

4144 South Tamiami Trail
941-921-4605
waltsfishmarketrestaurant.com

SOUTH TRAIL	SEAFOOD	COST: $$

HOURS: Daily, 11AM to 9PM • Market, 9AM to 8PM
Chickee Bar, 11AM to 11PM

WHAT TO EXPECT: Restaurant & market • Live music • Casual dining
Busy in season • Since 1918!

CARRYOUT/DELIVERY INFO: Full menu available for carryout.
Curbside pick up. Delivery not available.

SCAN FOR MENU

SOME BASICS

Reservations:	NO
Spirits:	FULL BAR
Parking:	LOT
Outdoor Dining:	YES

WATERFRONT

7660 South Tamiami Trail
941-921-1916
waterfrontoo.com

SOUTH TRAIL	AMERICAN	COST: $$$

HOURS: Dinner, Daily, 4PM to 10PM

WHAT TO EXPECT: Great casual steaks & seafood • Water view
An early dining crowd • Daily specials • Since 1986

CARRYOUT/DELIVERY INFO: Full menu available for carryout.
Curbside and contactless pick up. Delivery not available.

SCAN FOR MENU

SOME BASICS

Reservations:	YES
Spirits:	FULL BAR
Parking:	LOT
Outdoor Dining:	YES

WICKED CANTINA

1603 North Tamiami Trail*
941-706-2395
wickedcantina.com

NORTH TRAIL	TEX MEX	COST: $$

HOURS: Daily, 11AM to 10PM

WHAT TO EXPECT: Casual dining • Convenient before a show
Busy in season • Happy Hour daily

CARRYOUT/DELIVERY INFO: Online ordering. Full menu available
for carryout. Curbside pick up. No delivery available.

SCAN FOR MENU

SOME BASICS

Reservations:	YES
Spirits:	FULL BAR
Parking:	LOT
Outdoor Dining:	NO

LOCAL FARMERS MARKET INFORMATION

SARASOTA FARMERS MARKET
Lemon Avenue
Downtown Sarasota
Saturdays (Year Round)
7AM to 1PM
Rain or Shine
70+ Vendors
sarasotafarmersmarket.org

BRADENTON FARMERS MARKET
Old Main Street (12 St. W)
Saturdays (October thru May)
9AM to 2PM
realizebradenton.com/farmers_market

SIESTA KEY FARMERS MARKET
Davidson's Plaza (5124 Ocean Boulevard)
Sundays (Year Round)
9AM to 1PM
Rain or Shine
siestakeyfarmersmarket.org

PHILLIPPI FARMHOUSE MARKET
Phillippi Estates Park (5500 South Tamiami Trail)
Wednesdays (October thru April)
9AM to 2PM
35+ Vendors
farmhousemarket.org

VENICE FARMERS MARKET
Downtown Venice (Tampa Ave. & Nokomis Ave.)
Saturdays (Year Round)
8AM to 12PM
thevenicefarmersmarket.com

WHAT'S IN SEASON?

Our Sarasota area farmer's markets really give locals and visitors a taste of fresh Florida flavor. But, our markets are more than a place just to stock up for the week. They're a place to mingle with friends, enjoy some music or catch up on the latest neighborhood news!

Now you have good list of places to buy the freshest locally grown produce. But, what's the best time of year to enjoy Florida's fruits and vegetables? When are they at their peak of freshness? Here's a little help.

WINTER > Bell Pepper • Eggplant • Grapefruit
Strawberries • Squash • Tomatoes • Arugula • Kale
SPRING > Cantaloupe • Guava • Lettuce • Mushrooms
Oranges • Papaya • Radish • Swiss Chard • Strawberries
SUMMER > Avocado • Guava • Mango • Eggplant
Peanuts • Sweet Corn • Watermelon • Snow Peas
FALL > Cucumber • Grapefruit • Mushrooms • Lettuce
Snap Beans • Tangerines • Tomatoes • Peppers

We have super fresh seafood here in Sarasota. You can usually find a plentiful supply of grouper, red snapper, pompano, and mahi at our farmers markets. Of course, you can always find fresh Gulf shrimp in a variety of sizes.

The most anticipated seafood season runs from October 15th through May 15th. That's stone crab season! You're best off to grab these tasty delights towards the beginning of season when they're the most plentiful.

WORD OF MOUTH

6604 Gateway Avenue
941-925-2400
originalwordofmouth.com

GULF GATE	AMERICAN	COST: $$

HOURS: Daily, 8AM to 2PM

WHAT TO EXPECT: Daily specials • Casual dining • Good for families

CARRYOUT/DELIVERY INFO: Online ordering. Full menu available for carryout. Curbside and contactless pick up.
Delivery not available.

SCAN FOR MENU

SOME BASICS

Reservations:	NO
Spirits:	BEER/WINE
Parking:	LOT/STREET
Outdoor Dining:	NO

YODER'S RESTAURANT

3434 Bahia Vista Street
941-955-7771
yodersrestaurant.com

PINECRAFT	AMISH	COST: $

HOURS: Mon-Sat, 7AM to 8PM • CLOSED SUNDAY

WHAT TO EXPECT: Great for families • Easy on the wallet
Busy in season • Fantastic service • Pie!!

CARRYOUT/DELIVERY INFO: Online ordering. Full menu available for carryout and delivery. Delivery through Bite Squad.

SCAN FOR MENU

SOME BASICS

Reservations:	NO
Spirits:	NONE
Parking:	LOT
Outdoor Dining:	NO

YUME SUSHI
1532 Main Street
941-363-0604
yumerestaurant.com

DOWNTOWN	SUSHI	COST: $$

HOURS: Lunch, Mon-Sat, 11:30AM to 2PM
Dinner, Mon-Sun, 5PM to Close

WHAT TO EXPECT: Great for a date • Fun dining experience
Great sake selection

CARRYOUT/DELIVERY INFO: Full menu available for carryout and
delivery. Curbside pick up. Delivery available through Bite Squad.

SCAN FOR MENU

SOME BASICS
Reservations:	6 OR MORE
Spirits:	BEER/WINE
Parking:	STREET
Outdoor Dining:	NO

YUMMY HOUSE
1737 South Tamiami Trail
941-351-1688
yummyhouseflorida.com

SOUTH TRAIL	ASIAN	COST: $$

HOURS: Lunch, Daily, 11AM to 2:30PM • Dim Sum, 11AM to 2:30PM
Dinner, Mon-Sat, 5PM to 9:30PM • Sun, 5PM to 9PM

WHAT TO EXPECT: Busy in season • Lively atmosphere
Lots of parking

CARRYOUT/DELIVERY INFO: Online ordering. Full menu available
for carryout and delivery. Delivery through DoorDash.

SCAN FOR MENU

SOME BASICS
Reservations:	YES
Spirits:	FULL BAR
Parking:	LOT
Outdoor Dining:	NO

Restaurant Name	Address	Phone #
A Sprig of Thyme	1962 Hillview St	330-8890
Andrea's	2085 Siesta Dr	951-9200
Anna Maria Oyster Bar	6696 Cortez Rd	792-0077
Anna Maria Oyster Bar	1525 51st Ave E	721-7773
Antoine's Restaurant	5020 Fruitville Rd	377-2020
Apollonia Grill	8235 Cooper Creek	359-4816
Athen's Restaurant	2300 Bee Ridge Rd	706-4121
Avli Mess Hall	1592 Main St	365-2234
Baker & Wife	2157 Siesta Dr	960-1765
Bavaro's Pizza	27 Fletcher Ave	552-9131
Beach Bistro	6600 Gulf Dr N	778-6444
Beach House Restaurant	200 Gulf Dr N	779-2222
Bevardi's Salute!	23 N Lemon Ave	365-1020
Big Water Fish Market	6641 Midgnight Pass	554-8101
Bijou Café	1287 First St	366-8111
Blasé Southern Style	1920 Hillview St.	312-6850
Blu Kouzina	25 N Blvd of Pres	388-2619
Boca Kitchen, Bar, Mkt	21 S Lemon Ave	256-3565
The Bodhi Tree	1938 Adams Ln	702-8552
Bonjour French Cafe	5214 Ocean Blvd	346-0600
Brick's Smoked Meats	1528 State St	993-1435
Bridge Street Bistro	111 Gulf Dr S	782-1122
Bridges Restaurant	202 N Tamiami Trl	256-0190
Brine Seafood	2250 Gulf Gate Dr	404-5639
Burns Court Cafe	401 S Pineapple Ave	312-6633
Bushido Izayaki	3688 Webber St	217-5635

Restaurant Name	Address	Phone #
Café Baci	4001 S Tamiami Trl	921-4848
Café Barbosso	5501 Palmer Crossing	922-7999
Café Epicure	1298 Main St	366-5648
Café Gabbiano	5104 Ocean Blvd	349-1423
Cafe in the Park	2010 Adams Ln	361-3032
Café L'Europe	431 St Armands Cir	388-4415
Café Longet	239 Miami Ave W	244-2643
Café Venice	101 W Venice Ave	484-1855
Capt. Brian's Seafood	8421 N Tamiami Trl	351-4492
Capt. Curt's Oyster Bar	1200 Old Stickney Pt	349-3885
Caragiulos	69 S Palm Ave	951-0866
Casey Key Fish House	801 Blackburn Pt Rd	966-1901
Cassariano Italian Eat.	313 W Venice Ave	485-0507
C'est La Vie!	1553 Main St	906-9575
Cha Cha Coconuts	417 St Armands Cir	388-3300
Chianti Ristorante	3900 Clark Rd	952-3186
Circo	1435 2nd St	253-0978
Clasico Italian Chophse	1341 Main St	957-0700
The Columbia	411 St Armands Cir	388-3987
Connors Steakhouse	3501 S Tamiami Trl	260-3232
The Cottage	153 Avenida Messina	312-9300
Crab & Fin	420 St Armands Cir	388-3964
The Crow's Nest	1968 Tarpon Ctr Dr	484-9551
Curry Station	3550 Clark Rd	924-7222
Daiquiri Deck Raw Bar	5250 Ocean Blvd	349-8697
Daiquiri Deck Raw Bar	325 John Ringling Blvd	388-3325

Restaurant Name	Address	Phone #
Daiquiri Deck Raw Bar	300 W Venice Ave	488-0649
Daiquiri Deck Raw Bar	1250 Stickney Pt Rd	312-2422
DaRuMa Japanese	5459 Fruitville Rd	342-6600
DaRuMa Japanese	4910 S. Tamiami Trl	552-9465
Darwin Evolutionary	4141 S Tamiami Trl	260-5964
Demetrio's Pizzeria	4410 S Tamiami Trl	922-1585
Der Dutchman	3713 Bahia Vista	955-8007
Dolce Italia	6606 Superior Ave	921-7007
Drift Kitchen	700 Benjamin Franklin	388-2161
Drunken Poet Café	1572 Main St	955-8404
Dry Dock Waterfront	412 Gulf of Mexico Dr	383-0102
Dutch Valley Restaurant	6731 S Tamiami Trl	924-1770
Duval's, Fresh, Local...	1435 Main St	312-4001
El Toro Bravo	3218 Clark Rd	924-0006
Euphemia Haye	5540 Gulf of Mexico Dr	383-3633
EVOQ	1175 N. Gulfstream	260-8255
1592 Wood Fired Kitch	1592 Main St	365-2234
Fins At Sharkey's	1600 Harbor Dr S	999-3467
Flavio's Brick Oven	5239 Ocean Blvd	349-0995
Flavio's on Main	1766 Main St	960-2305
Fresh Catch Market	7119 S Tamiami Trl	413-7133
Fresh Start Cafe	630 S Orange Ave	373-1242
Fushipoke	128 N. Orange Ave	330-1795
Gecko's Grill & Pub	6606 S Tamiami Trl	248-2020
Gecko's Grill & Pub	5588 Palmer Crossing	923-6061
Gecko's Grill & Pub	351 N Cattlemen Rd	378-0077

Restaurant Name	Address	Phone #
Gecko's Grill & Pub	1900 Hillview St	953-2929
Gentile Cheesesteaks	7523 S Tamiami Trl	926-0441
Gilligan's Island Bar	5253 Ocean Blvd	349-4759
The Grasshopper	7253 S Tamiami Trl	923-3688
Grillsmith's	6240 S Tamiami Trl	259-8383
GROVE Restaurant	10670 Boardwalk Lp	893-4321
Gulf Gate Food & Beer	6528 Superior Ave	952-3361
Harry's Continental Kit.	525 St Judes Dr	383-0777
Hob Nob Drive-In	1701 Washington Blvd	955-5001
The Hub Baha Grill	5148 Ocean Blvd	349-6800
Ichiban Sushi	2724 Stickney Pt Rd	924-1611
Il Panificio	6630 Gateway Ave	921-5570
Indigenous	239 Links Ave	706-4740
Inkawasi Peruvian	10667 Boardwalk Lp	360-1110
Irish 31	3750 S Tamiami Trl	234-9265
Island House Tap & Grl.	5110 Ocean Blvd	312-9205
Jack Dusty	1111 Ritz-Carlton Dr	309-2266
Jpan Sushi & Grill	3 Paradise Plaza	954-5726
Jpan Sushi & Grill	229 N Cattlemen Rd	954-5726
JR's Old Packinghouse	987 S Packinghse Rd	371-9358
Kacey's Seafood	4904 Fruitville Rd	378-3644
Karl Ehmer's Alpine	4520 S Tamiami Trl	922-3797
Kiyoski's Sushi	6550 Gateway Ave	924-3781
Knick's Tavern & Grill	1818 S Osprey Ave	955-7761
La Dolce Vita	2704 Stickney Pt Rd	210-3631
Lazy Lobster	5350 Gulf of Mexico Dr	388-0440

Restaurant Name	Address	Phone #
Lazy Lobster	7602 N Lockwood Rg	351-5515
Le Colonne Ristorante	22 S Blvd of the Pres	388-4348
Libby's	1917 S Osprey Ave	487-7300
Lila	1576 Main St	296-1042
The Lobster Pot	5157 Ocean Blvd	349-2323
Lovely Square	6559 Gateway Ave	724-2512
Made	1990 Main St	953-2900
Madfish Grill	4059 Cattlemen Rd	377-3474
Mademoiselle Paris	8527 Cooper Creek Bl	355-2323
Madison Avenue Deli	28 N Blvd of President	388-3354
Main Bar Sandwich Shp	1944 Main St	955-8733
Main Street Trattoria	8131 Lakewood Main	907-1518
Maison Blanche	2605 Gulf of Mexico Dr	383-8088
Mandeville Beer Garden	428 N Lemon Ave	954-8688
Mar-Vista Restaurant	760 Broadway St	383-2391
Marcello's Ristorante	4155 S Tamiami Trl	921-6794
Marina Jack's	2 Marina Plaza	365-4243
Mattison's City Grille	1 N Lemon Ave	330-0440
Mattison's Forty One	7275 S Tamiami Trl	921-3400
Mediterraneo	1970 Main St	365-4122
Melange	1568 Main St	953-7111
Mellie's New York Deli	4650 St Rd 64 - BTON	281-2139
Mi Pueblo	4436 Bee Ridge Rd	379-2880
Mi Pueblo	4804 Tuttle Ave	359-9303
Michael's On East	1212 East Ave	366-0007
Michelle's Brown Bag	1819 Main St	365-5858

Restaurant Name	Address	Phone #
Miguel's	6631 Midnight Pass	349-4024
Millie's Cafe	3900 Clark Rd	923-4054
Monk's Steamer Bar	6690 Superior Ave	927-3388
Munchies 420 Café	6639 Superior Ave	929-9893
99 Bottles Taproom	1445 2nd St	487-7874
Nancy's Bar-B-Que	14475 SR 70	999-2390
Napule Ristorante	7129 S Tamiami Trl	556-9639
Nellie's Deli	15 S Beneva Rd	924-2705
New Pass Grill	1505 Ken Thompson	388-3050
Oak & Stone	5405 University Pkwy	225-4590
Oak & Stone	4067 Clark Rd	893-4881
Oasis Café	3542 S Osprey Ave	957-1214
Off The Hook Seafood	6630 Gateway Ave	923-5570
The Old Salty Dog	5023 Ocean Blvd	349-0158
The Old Salty Dog	160 Ken Thompson Pk	388-4311
The Old Salty Dog	1485 S Tamiami Trl	483-1000
O'Leary's Tiki Bar	5 Bayfront Dr	953-7505
Opa Opa	6525 Superior Ave	927-1672
Ophelia's on the Bay	9105 Midnight Pass	349-2212
Origin Beer & Pizza	3837 Hillview St	316-9222
Origin Beer & Pizza	5070 Clark Rd	217-6533
Ortygia	1418 13th Street W	741-8646
The Overton	1420 Blvd of the Arts	500-9175
Owen's Fish Camp	516 Burns Ct	951-6936
Pacific Rim	1859 Hillview St	330-8071
Parrot Patio Bar & Grill	3602 Webber St	952-3352
Pascone's Ristorante	5239 University Pkwy	210-7268

Restaurant Name	Address	Phone #
Pastry Art Bakery	1512 Main St	955-7545
Patrick's 1481	1481 Main St	955-1481
Pazzo Southside	1936 Hillview St	260-8831
Phillippi Creek Oyster	5363 S Tamiami Trl	925-4444
Pho Cali	1578 Main St	955-2683
Piccolo Italian Market	6518 Gateway Ave	923-2202
Pier 22	1200 1st Avenue W	748-8087
The Point	135 Bayview Dr	218-6114
Pop's Sunset Grill	112 Circuit Rd	488-3177
Pub 32	8383 S Tamiami Trl	952-3070
Rasoi Indian Kitchen	7119 S Tamiami Trl	921-9200
Reef Cakes	1812 S Osprey Ave	444-7968
Rendez-Vous Bakery	5336 Clark Rd	924-1234
Reyna's Taqueria	935 N Beneva Rd	260-8343
Rick's French Bistro	2177 Siesta Dr	957-0533
Rico's Pizza - Bay Rd	1902 Bay Rd	366-8988
Roessler's	2033 Vamo Way	966-5688
Rosebud's Steakhouse	2215 S Tamiami Trl	918-8771
The Rosemary	411 N Orange Ave	955-7600
Rosemary & Thyme	511 N Orange Ave	955-7600
Sage	1216 1st St	445-5660
The Sandbar	100 Spring Ave	778-0444
Sarasota Brewing Comp	6607 Gateway Ave	925-2337
Sardinia	5770 S Tamiami Trl	702-8582
Schnitzel Kitchen	6521 Superior Ave	922-9299
Screaming Goat Taq.	6606 Superior Ave	210-3992

Restaurant Name	Address	Phone #
Seabar	6540 Superior Ave	923-6605
Selva Grill	1345 Main St	362-4427
Shakespeare's Eng. Pub	3550 S Osprey Ave	364-5938
Shaner's Pizza	6500 Superior Ave	927-2708
Sharkey's on the Pier	1600 Harbor Dr S	488-1456
Shore Diner	465 John Ringling	296-0303
Siegfried's Restaurant	1869 Fruitville Rd	330-9330
Siesta Key Oyster Bar	5238 Ocean Blvd	346-5443
Simon's Coffee House	5900 S Tamiami Trl	926-7151
Smoqehouse	6112 S Tamiami Trl	923-9090
Snook Haven	500 E Venice Ave	485-7221
S Philly Cheesesteaks	1439 Main St	330-8208
Southside Deli	1825 Hillview St	330-9302
Speaks Clam Bar	29 N Blvd of Pres.	232-7633
Spear Fish Grille	1265 Old Stickney Pt	349-1970
Spice Station	1438 Blvd of the Arts	343-2894
Star Thai & Sushi	935 N Beneva Rd	706-3848
Star Thai & Sushi	240 Avenida Madera	217-6758
State St. Eating House	1533 State St	951-1533
Station 400	400 Lemon Ave	906-1400
Station 400	8215 Lakewood Main	907-0648
Station 400	4910 S Tamiami Trl	927-0402
Stottlemeyer's Smokehs	19 East Rd	312-5969
Summer House	149 Avenida Messina	206-2675
Sun Garden Café	210 Avenida Madera	346-7170
Sunnyside Cafe	4900 N Tamiami Trl	359-9500

Restaurant Name	Address	Phone #
Tamiami Tap	711 S Osprey Ave	500-3182
Tandoor	8453 Cooper Creek	926-3070
Taste of Asia	4413 S Tamiami Trl	923-2742
Tasty Home Cookin'	3854 S Tuttle Ave	921-4969
Toasted Mango Café	430 N Tamiami Trl	388-7728
Toasted Mango Café	6621 Midnight Pass	552-6485
Tommy Bahama Café	300 John Ringling Blvd	388-2888
Tony's Chicago Beef	6569 Superior Ave	922-7979
Turtle's	8875 Midnight Pass	346-2207
Valentino's Pizzeria	4045 Clark Rd	921-9600
Valentino's Pizzeria	9203 Cooper Creek	349-6400
Veg	2164 Gulf Gate Dr	312-6424
Venezia	373 St Armands Cir	388-1400
Veronica Fish & Oyster	1830 S Osprey Ave	366-1342
Viento Kitchen + Bar	4711 Gulf of Mexico Dr	248-1211
Village Café	5133 Ocean Blvd	349-2822
Walt's Fish Market	4144 S Tamiami Trl	921-4605
Waterfront	7660 S Tamiami Trl	921-1916
Wicked Cantina	1603 N Tamiami Trl	821-2990
Word of Mouth	6604 Gateway Ave	925-2400
Yoder's Restaurant	3434 Bahia Vista	955-7771
Yume Sushi	1532 Main St	363-0604
Yummy House	1737 S Tamiami Trl	351-1688

AMERICAN		
Restaurant Name	Address	Phone #
Baker & Wife	2157 Siesta Dr	960-1765
Beach Bistro	6600 Gulf Dr N	778-6444
Beach House Rest.	200 Gulf Dr N	779-2222
Bijou Café	1287 First St	366-8111
Blasé Southern Style	1920 Hillview St.	312-6850
Boca Kitchen, Bar, Mkt.	21 S. Lemon Ave	256-3565
Brick's Smoked Meats	1528 State St	993-1435
Bridge Street Bistro	111 Gulf Dr S	782-1122
Bridges Restaurant	202 N Tamiami Trl	256-0190
Burns Court Cafe	401 S Pineapple Ave	312-6633
Café Venice	101 W Venice Ave	484-1855
Cha Cha Coconuts	417 St Armands Cir	388-3300
The Cottage	153 Avenida Messina	312-9300
Daiquiri Deck Raw Bar	5250 Ocean Blvd	349-8697
Daiquiri Deck Raw Bar	325 John Ringling Blvd	388-3325
Daiquiri Deck Raw Bar	300 W Venice Ave	488-0649
Daiquiri Deck Raw Bar	1250 Stickney Pt Rd	312-2422
Der Dutchman	3713 Bahia Vista	955-8007
Drift Kitchen	700 Benjamin Franklin	388-2161
Dutch Valley Restaurant	6731 S Tamiami Trl	924-1770
Euphemia Haye	5540 Gulf of Mexico Dr	383-3633
EVOQ	1175 N. Gulfstream	260-8255
Fresh Start Cafe	630 S Orange Ave	373-1242
Gecko's Grill & Pub	6606 S Tamiami Trl	248-2020
Gecko's Grill & Pub	1900 Hillview St	953-2929

AMERICAN		
Restaurant Name	Address	Phone #
Gecko's Grill & Pub	5588 Palmer Crossing	923-6061
Gecko's Grill & Pub	351 N Cattlemen Rd	378-0077
Gentile Cheesesteaks	7523 S Tamiami Trl	926-0441
Gilligan's Island Bar	5253 Ocean Blvd	349-4759
Grillsmith's	6240 S Tamiami Trl	259-8383
GROVE Restaurant	10670 Boardwalk Lp	893-4321
Gulf Gate Food & Beer	6528 Superior Ave	952-3361
Harry's Continental Kit.	525 St Judes Dr	383-0777
Hob Nob Drive-In	1701 Washington Blvd	955-5001
The Hub Baha Grill	5148 Ocean Blvd	349-6800
Indigenous	239 Links Ave	706-4740
Island House Tap & Grl.	5110 Ocean Blvd	312-9205
Jack Dusty	1111 Ritz-Carlton Dr	309-2266
JR's Old Packinghouse	987 S Packinghouse	371-9358
Knick's Tavern & Grill	1818 S Osprey Ave	955-7761
Libby's	1917 S Osprey Ave	487-7300
Lila	1576 Main St	296-1042
Lovely Square	6559 Gateway Ave	724-2512
Made	1990 Main St	953-2900
Madfish Grill	4059 Cattlemen Rd	377-3474
Mandeville Beer Garden	428 N Lemon Ave	954-8688
Mar-Vista Restaurant	760 Broadway St	383-2391
Mattison's City Grille	1 N Lemon Ave	330-0440
Mattison's Forty One	7275 S Tamiami Trl	921-3400
Melange	1568 Main St	953-7111

AMERICAN		
Restaurant Name	**Address**	**Phone #**
Michael's On East	1212 East Ave	366-0007
Millie's Cafe	3900 Clark Rd	923-4054
Munchies 420 Café	6639 Superior Ave	929-9893
99 Bottles Taproom	1445 2nd St	487-7874
Nancy's Bar-B-Que	14475 SR 70	999-2390
New Pass Grill	1505 Ken Thompson	388-3050
Oak & Stone	5405 University Pkwy	225-4590
Oak & Stone	4067 Clark Rd	893-4881
Oasis Cafe	3542 S Osprey Ave	957-1214
The Old Salty Dog	5023 Ocean Blvd	349-0158
The Old Salty Dog	160 Ken Thompson Pk	388-4311
The Old Salty Dog	1485 S Tamiami Trl	483-1000
O'Leary's Tiki Bar	5 Bayfront Dr	953-7505
Ophelia's on the Bay	9105 Midnight Pass	349-2212
The Overton	1420 Blvd of the Arts	500-9175
Parrot Patio Bar & Grill	3602 Webber St	952-3352
Pastry Art Bakery	1512 Main St	955-7545
Patrick's 1481	1481 Main St	955-1481
The Point	135 Bayview Dr	218-6114
Pop's Sunset Grill	112 Circuit Rd	488-3177
The Rosemary	411 N Orange Ave	955-7600
Rosemary & Thyme	511 N Orange Ave	955-7600
Sage	1216 1st St	445-5660
Sarasota Brewing Comp	6607 Gateway Ave	925-2337
Sharkey's on the Pier	1600 Harbor Dr S	488-1456
Shore Diner	465 John Ringling Blvd	296-0303

AMERICAN		
Restaurant Name	Address	Phone #
Smoqehouse	6112 S Tamiami Trl	923-9090
Snook Haven	500 E Venice Ave	485-7221
Siesta Key Oyster Bar	5238 Ocean Blvd	346-5443
State St. Eating House	1533 State St	951-1533
Station 400	400 Lemon Ave	906-1400
Station 400	8215 Lakewood Main	907-0648
Station 400	4832 S Tamiami Trl	927-0402
Stottlemeyer's Smokehs	19 East Rd	312-5969
Sun Garden Cafe	210 Avenida Madera	346-7170
Sunnyside Cafe	4900 N Tamiami Trl	359-9500
Tamiami Tap	711 S Osprey Ave	500-3182
Tasty Home Cookin'	3854 S Tuttle Ave	921-4969
Toasted Mango Café	6621 Midnight Pass	552-6485
Toasted Mango Café	430 N Tamiami Trl	388-7728
Tommy Bahama Café	300 John Ringling Blvd	388-2888
Tony's Chicago Beef	6569 Superior Ave	922-7979
Turtle's	8875 Midnight Pass	346-2207
Veg	2164 Gulf Gate Dr	312-6424
Viento Kitchen + Bar	4711 Gulf of Mexico Dr	248-1211
Village Café	5133 Ocean Blvd	349-2822
Waterfront	7660 S Tamiami Trl	921-1916
Word of Mouth	6604 Gateway Ave	925-2400
Yoder's Restaurant	3434 Bahia Vista	955-7771
ASIAN		
Bushido Izayaki	3688 Webber St	217-5635

ASIAN		
Restaurant Name	Address	Phone #
Drunken Poet Café	1572 Main St	955-8404
DaRuMa Japanese	5459 Fruitville Rd	342-6600
DaRuMa Japanese	4910 S. Tamiami Trl	552-9465
Fushipoke	128 N. Orange Ave	330-1795
Ichiban Sushi	2724 Stickney Pt Rd	924-1611
Jpan Sushi & Grill	3 Paradise Plaza	954-5726
Jpan Sushi & Grill	229 N Cattlemen Rd	954-5726
Kiyoski's Sushi	6550 Gateway Ave	924-3781
Pacific Rim	1859 Hillview St	330-8071
Pho Cali	1578 Main St	955-2683
Seabar	6540 Superior Ave	923-6605
Spice Station	1438 Blvd of the Arts	343-2894
Star Thai & Sushi	935 N Beneva Rd	706-3848
Star Thai & Sushi	240 Avenida Madera	217-6758
Taste of Asia	4413 S Tamiami Trl	923-2742
Yume Sushi	1532 Main St	363-0604
Yummy House	1737 S Tamiami Trl	351-1688

CUBAN, MEXICAN & SPANISH		
Circo	1435 2nd St	253-0978
The Columbia	411 St Armands Cir	388-3987
El Toro Bravo	2720 Stickney Pt Rd	924-0006
The Grasshopper	7253 S Tamiami Trl	923-3688
Mi Pueblo	4804 Tuttle Ave	359-9303
Reyna's Taqueria	935 N Beneva Rd	260-8343
Screaming Goat Taq.	6606 Superior Ave	210-3992
Wicked Cantina	1603 N Tamiami Trl	821-2990

DELI

Restaurant Name	Address	Phone #
Cafe in the Park	2010 Adams Ln	361-3032
Gentile Cheesesteaks	7523 S Tamiami Trl	926-0441
Madison Avenue Deli	28 N Blvd of President	388-3354
Main Bar Sandwich Shp	1944 Main St	955-8733
Mellie's New York Deli	4650 St Rd 64 - BTON	281-2139
Michelle's Brown Bag	1819 Main St	365-5858
Nellie's Deli	15 S Beneva Rd	924-2705
Piccolo Italian Market	6518 Gateway Ave	923-2202
Simon's Coffee House	5900 S Tamiami Trl	926-7151
Southside Deli	1825 Hillview St	330-9302
S Philly Cheesesteaks	1439 Main St	330-8208

ENGLISH, IRISH & SCOTTISH

Irish 31	3750 S Tamiami Trl	234-9265
Pub 32	8383 S Tamiami Trl	952-3070
Shakespeare's Eng Pub	3550 S Osprey Ave	364-5938

FRENCH

A Sprig of Thyme	1962 Hillview St	330-8890
Bonjour French Cafe	5214 Ocean Blvd	346-0600
C'est La Vie!	1553 Main St	906-9575
Café Longet	239 Miami Ave W	244-2643
Mademoiselle Paris	8527 Cooper Creek Bl	355-2323
Maison Blanche	2605 Gulf of Mexico Dr	383-8088
Miguel's	6631 Midnight Pass	349-4024
Rendez-Vous Bakery	5336 Clark Rd	924-1234
Rick's French Bistro	2177 Siesta Dr	957-0533

GREEK		
Restaurant Name	**Address**	**Phone #**
Apollonia Grill	8235 Cooper Creek	359-4816
Blu Kouzina	25 N Blvd of Pres	388-2619
1592 Wood Fired Kitch	1592 Main St	365-2234
Opa Opa	6525 Superior Ave	927-1672

INDIAN		
Curry Station	3550 Clark Rd	924-7222
Rasoi Indian Kitchen	7119 S Tamiami Trl	921-9200
Tandoor	8453 Cooper Creek	926-3070

ITALIAN		
Andrea's	2085 Siesta Dr	951-9200
Bavaro's Pizza	27 Fletcher Ave	552-9131
Bevardi's Salute!	23 N Lemon Ave	365-1020
Cafe Baci	4001 S. Tamiami Trl	921-4848
Café Barbosso	5501 Palmer Crossing	922-7999
Café Epicure	1298 Main St	366-5648
Café Gabbiano	5104 Ocean Blvd	349-1423
Café L'Europe	431 St Armands Cir	388-4415
Caragiulos	69 S Palm Ave	951-0866
Cassariano Italian Eat.	313 W Venice Ave	485-0507
Chianti Ristorante	3900 Clark Rd	952-3186
Clasico Italian Chophse	1341 Main St	957-0700
Demetrio's Pizzeria	4410 S Tamiami Trl	922-1585
Dolce Italia	6606 Superior Ave	921-7007
Flavio's Brick Oven	5239 Ocean Blvd	349-0995

ITALIAN		
Restaurant Name	Address	Phone #
Flavio's on Main	1766 Main St	960-2305
Il Panificio	1703 Main St	366-5570
La Dolce Vita	2704 Stickney Pt Rd	210-3631
Le Colonne Ristorante	22 S Blvd of the Pres	388-4348
Main Street Trattoria	8131 Lakewood Main	907-1518
Marcello's Ristorante	4155 S Tamiami Trl	921-6794
Mediterraneo	1970 Main St	365-4122
Napule Ristorante	7129 S Tamiami Trl	556-9639
Pascone's Ristorante	5239 University Pkwy	210-7268
Pazzo Southside	1936 Hillview St	260-8831
Piccolo Italian Market	6518 Gateway Ave	923-2202
Sardinia	5770 S Tamiami Trl	702-8582
Shaner's Pizza	6500 Superior Ave	927-2708
Valentino's Pizzeria	4045 Clark Rd	921-9600
Valentino's Pizzeria	9203 Cooper Creek	349-6400
Venezia	373 St Armands Cir	388-1400

SEAFOOD		
Anna Maria Oyster Bar	6906 14th St W	758-7880
Anna Maria Oyster Bar	6696 Cortez Rd	792-0077
Big Water Fish Market	6641 Midgnight Pass	554-8101
Brine Seafood	2250 Gulf Gate Dr	404-5639
Capt. Brian's Seafood	8421 N Tamiami Trl	351-4492
Capt. Curt's Oyster Bar	1200 Old Stickney Pt	349-3885

SEAFOOD		
Restaurant Name	**Address**	**Phone #**
Casey Key Fish House	801 Blackburn Pt Rd	966-1901
Crab & Fin	420 St Armands Cir	388-3964
The Crow's Nest	1968 Tarpon Ctr Dr	484-9551
Dry Dock Waterfront	412 Gulf of Mexico Dr	383-0102
Duval's, Fresh, Local...	1435 Main St	312-4001
Fins At Sharkey's	1600 Harbor Dr S	999-3467
Fresh Catch Market	7119 S Tamiami Trl	413-7133
Kacey's Seafood	4904 Fruitville Rd	378-3644
Lazy Lobster	5350 Gulf of Mexico Dr	388-0440
Lazy Lobster	7602 N Lockwood Rg	351-5515
The Lobster Pot	5157 Ocean Blvd	349-2323
Mar-Vista Restaurant	760 Broadway St	383-2391
Marina Jack's	2 Marina Plaza	365-4243
Monk's Steamer Bar	6690 Superior Ave	927-3388
Off The Hook Seafood	6630 Gateway Ave	923-5570
Owen's Fish Camp	516 Burns Ct	951-6936
Phillippi Creek Oyster	5363 S Tamiami Trl	925-4444
Pier 22	1200 1st Avenue W	748-8087
Reef Cakes	1812 S Osprey Ave	444-7968
The Sandbar	100 Spring Ave	778-0444
Seabar	6540 Superior Ave	923-6605
Siesta Key Oyster Bar	5238 Ocean Blvd	346-5443
Speaks Clam Bar	29 N Blvd of Pres.	232-7633
Spear Fish Grille	1265 Old Stickney Pt	349-1970
Veronica Fish & Oyster	1830 S Osprey Ave	366-1342
Walt's Fish Market	4144 S Tamiami Trl	921-4605

STEAKHOUSE		
Restaurant Name	**Address**	**Phone #**
Connors Steakhouse	3501 S Tamiami Trl	260-3232
Fleming's Steakhouse	2001 Siesta Dr	358-9463
Karl Ehmer's Alpine	4520 S Tamiami Trl	922-3797
Rosebud's Steakhouse	2215 S Tamiami Trl	918-8771
Ruth's Chris Steakhouse	6700 S Tamiami Trl	942-9442
Summer House	149 Avenida Messina	206-2675

ANNA MARIA, BRADENTON, & PALMETTO		
Beach Bistro	6600 Gulf Dr N	778-6444
The Beach House	200 Gulf Dr N	779-2222
Bridge Street Bistro	111 Gulf Dr S	782-1122
Mellie's New York Deli	4650 St Rd 64 - BTON	281-2139
Ortygia	1418 13th Street W	741-8646
Pier 22	1200 1st Avenue W	748-8087
The Sandbar	100 Spring Ave	778-0444

DOWNTOWN		
Bavaro's Pizza	27 Fletcher Ave	552-9131
Bevardi's Salute!	23 N Lemon Ave	365-1020
Bijou Cafe	1287 First St	366-8111
Boca Kitchen, Bar, Mkt	21 S Lemon Ave	256-3565
The Bodhi Tree	1938 Adams Ln	702-8552

DOWNTOWN		
Restaurant Name	**Address**	**Phone #**
Brick's Smoked Meats	1528 State St	993-1435
Bridges Restaurant	202 N Tamiami Trl	256-0190
Burns Court Cafe	401 S Pineapple Ave	312-6633
Café Epicure	1298 Main St	366-5648
Cafe in the Park	2010 Adams Ln	361-3032
Caragiulos	69 S Palm Ave	951-0866
C'est La Vie!	1553 Main St	906-9575
Circo	1435 2nd St	253-0978
Clasico Italian Chophse	1341 Main St	957-0700
Drunken Poet Café	1572 Main St	955-8404
Duval's, Fresh, Local...	1435 Main St	312-4001
EVOQ	1175 N. Gulfstream	260-8255
1592 Wood Fired Kitch	1592 Main St	365-2234
Flavio's on Main	1766 Main St	960-2305
Fresh Start Cafe	630 S Orange Ave	373-1242
Fushipoke	128 N. Orange Ave	330-1795
Il Panificio	1703 Main St	366-5570
Indigenous	239 Links Ave	706-4740
Jack Dusty	1111 Ritz-Carlton Dr	309-2266
Lila	1576 Main St	296-1042
Made	1990 Main St	953-2900
Main Bar Sandwich Shp	1944 Main St	955-8733
Mandeville Beer Garden	428 N Lemon Ave	954-8688
Marina Jack's	2 Marina Plaza	365-4243

DOWNTOWN		
Restaurant Name	Address	Phone #
Mattison's City Grille	1 N Lemon Ave	330-0440
Mediterraneo	1970 Main St	365-4122
Melange	1568 Main St	953-7111
Michelle's Brown Bag	1819 Main St	365-5858
99 Bottles Taproom	1445 2nd St	487-7874
O'Leary's Tiki Bar	5 Bayfront Dr	953-7505
The Overton	1420 Blvd of the Arts	500-9175
Owen's Fish Camp	516 Burns Ct	951-6936
Pastry Art Bakery	1512 Main St	955-7545
Patrick's 1481	1481 Main St	955-1481
Pho Cali	1578 Main St	955-2683
The Rosemary	411 N Orange Ave	955-7600
Rosemary & Thyme	511 N Orange Ave	955-7600
Sage	1216 1st St	445-5660
Selva Grill	1345 Main St	362-4427
Siegfried's Restaurant	1869 Fruitville Rd	330-9330
S Philly Cheesesteaks	1439 Main St	330-8208
Spice Station	1438 Blvd of the Arts	343-2894
State St Eating House	1533 State St	951-1533
Station 400	400 Lemon Ave	906-1400
Tamiami Tap	711 S Osprey Ave	500-3182
Toasted Mango Café	430 N Tamiami Trl	388-7728
Wicked Cantina	1603 N Tamiami Trl	821-2990
Yume Sushi	1532 Main St	363-0604

GULF GATE		
Restaurant Name	**Address**	**Phone #**
Brine Seafood	2250 Gulf Gate Dr	404-5639
Dolce Italia	6606 Superior Ave	921-7007
Gulf Gate Food & Beer	6528 Superior Ave	952-3361
Ichiban Sushi	2724 Stickney Pt Rd	924-1611
Kiyoski's Sushi	6550 Gateway Ave	924-3781
Lovely Square	6559 Gateway Ave	724-2512
Monk's Steamer Bar	6690 Superior Ave	927-3388
Munchies 420 Café	6639 Superior Ave	929-9893
Off The Hook Seafood	6630 Gateway Ave	923-5570
Opa Opa	6525 Superior Ave	927-1672
Piccolo Italian Market	6518 Gateway Ave	923-2202
Sarasota Brewing Comp	6607 Gateway Ave	925-2337
Schnitzel Kitchen	6521 Superior Ave	922-9299
Seabar	6540 Superior Ave	923-6605
Screaming Goat Taq.	6606 Superior Ave	210-3992
Shaner's Pizza	6500 Superior Ave	927-2708
Tony's Chicago Beef	6569 Superior Ave	922-7979
Veg	2164 Gulf Gate Dr	312-6424
Word of Mouth	6604 Gateway Ave	925-2400

LONGBOAT KEY & LIDO KEY		
Drift Kitchen	700 Benjamin Franklin	388-2161
Dry Dock Waterfront	412 Gulf of Mexico Dr	383-0102
Euphemia Haye	5540 Gulf of Mexico Dr	383-3633

LONGBOAT KEY & LIDO KEY

Restaurant Name	Address	Phone #
Lazy Lobster	5350 Gulf of Mexico Dr	388-0440
Harry's Continental Kit.	525 St Judes Dr	383-0777
Maison Blanche	2605 Gulf of Mexico Dr	383-8088
Mar-Vista Restaurant	760 Broadway St	383-2391
New Pass Grill	1505 Ken Thompson	388-3050
Viento Kitchen + Bar	4711 Gulf of Mexico Dr	248-1211

LAKEWOOD RANCH & UNIVERSITY PARK

Apollonia Grill	8235 Cooper Creek	359-4816
GROVE Restaurant	10670 Boardwalk Lp	893-4321
Inkawasi Peruvian	10667 Boardwalk Lp	360-1110
Jpan Sushi & Grill	229 N Cattlemen Rd	954-5726
Mademoiselle Paris	8527 Cooper Creek Bl	355-2323
Main Street Trattoria	8131 Lakewood Main	907-1518
Nancy's Bar-B-Que	14475 SR 70	999-2390
Oak & Stone	5405 University Pkwy	225-4590
Pascone's Ristorante	5239 University Pkwy	210-7268
Tandoor	8453 Cooper Creek	926-3070

NORTH TAMIAMI TRAIL

Capt. Brian's Seafood	8421 N Tamiami Trl	351-4492
Hob Nob Drive-In	1701 Washington Blvd	955-5001
Sunnyside Cafe	4900 N Tamiami Trl	359-9500
Toasted Mango Café	430 N Tamiami Trl	388-7728
Wicked Cantina	1603 N Tamiami Trl	821-2990

ST. ARMANDS KEY		
Restaurant Name	Address	Phone #
Blu Kouzina	25 N Blvd of Pres	388-2619
Café L'Europe	431 St Armands Cir	388-4415
Cha Cha Coconuts	417 St Armands Cir	388-3300
The Columbia	411 St Armands Cir	388-3987
Crab & Fin	420 St Armands Cir	388-3964
Le Colonne Ristorante	22 S Blvd of the Pres	388-4348
Madison Avenue Deli	28 N Blvd of President	388-3354
Shore Diner	465 John Ringling Blvd	296-0303
Speaks Clam Bar	29 N Blvd of Pres	232-7633
Tommy Bahama Cafe	300 John Ringling Blvd	388-2888
Venezia	373 St Armands Cir	388-1400

SIESTA KEY		
Big Water Fish Market	6641 Midgnight Pass	554-8101
Bonjour French Cafe	5214 Ocean Blvd	346-0600
Café Gabbiano	5104 Ocean Blvd	349-1423
Capt. Curt's Oyster Bar	1200 Old Stickney Pt	349-3885
The Cottage	153 Avenida Messina	312-9300
Daiquiri Deck Raw Bar	5250 Ocean Blvd	349-8697
Flavio's Brick Oven	5239 Ocean Blvd	349-0995
Gilligan's Island Bar	5253 Ocean Blvd	349-4759
The Hub Baha Grill	5148 Ocean Blvd	349-6800
Island House Tap & Grl.	5110 Ocean Blvd	312-9205
The Lobster Pot	5157 Ocean Blvd	349-2323
Miguel's	6631 Midnight Pass	349-4024

SIESTA KEY		
Restaurant Name	**Address**	**Phone #**
The Old Salty Dog	5023 Ocean Blvd	349-0158
Ophelia's on the Bay	9105 Midnight Pass	349-2212
Siesta Key Oyster Bar	5238 Ocean Blvd	346-5443
Spear Fish Grille	1265 Old Stickney Pt	349-1970
Star Thai & Sushi	240 Avenida Madera	217-6758
Summer House	149 Avenida Messina	206-2675
Sun Garden Café	210 Avenida Madera	346-7170
Toasted Mango Café	6621 Midnight Pass	552-6485
Turtle's	8875 Midnight Pass	346-2207
Village Café	5133 Ocean Blvd	349-2822

SOUTH TAMIAMI TRAIL		
Cafe Baci	4001 S. Tamiami Trl	921-4848
DaRuMa Japanese	4910 S. Tamiami Trl	552-9465
Darwin Evolutionary	4141 S Tamiami Trl	260-5964
Demetrio's Pizzeria	4410 S Tamiami Trl	922-1585
Dutch Valley Restaurant	6731 S Tamiami Trl	924-1770
Fresh Catch Market	7119 S Tamiami Trl	413-7133
Gecko's Grill & Pub	4870 S Tamiami Trl	923-8896
Gentile Cheesesteaks	7523 S Tamiami Trl	926-0441
The Grasshopper	7253 S Tamiami Trl	923-3688
Grillsmith's	6240 S Tamiami Trl	259-8383
Irish 31	3750 S Tamiami Trl	234-9265
Karl Ehmer's Alpine	4520 S Tamiami Trl	922-3797
Marcello's Ristorante	4155 S Tamiami Trl	921-6794
Mattison's Forty One	7275 S Tamiami Trl	921-3400

SOUTH TAMIAMI TRAIL		
Restaurant Name	**Address**	**Phone #**
Michael's On East	1212 East Ave	366-0007
Napule Ristorante	7129 S Tamiami Trl	556-9639
Phillippi Creek Oyster	5363 S Tamiami Trl	925-4444
Pub 32	8383 S Tamiami Trl	952-3070
Rasoi Indian Kitchen	7119 S Tamiami Trl	921-9200
Roessler's	2033 Vamo Way	966-5688
Ruth's Chris Steakhouse	6700 S Tamiami Trl	942-9442
Sardinia	5770 S Tamiami Trl	702-8582
Simon's Coffee House	5900 S Tamiami Trl	926-7151
Smoqehouse	6112 S Tamiami Trl	923-9090
Taste of Asia	4413 S Tamiami Trl	923-2742
Walt's Fish Market	4144 S Tamiami Trl	921-4605
Waterfront	7660 S Tamiami Trl	921-1916
Yummy House	1737 S Tamiami Trl	351-1688

SOUTHSIDE VILLAGE		
A Sprig of Thyme	1962 Hillview St	330-8890
Blase Southern Style	1920 Hillview St.	312-6850
Knick's Tavern & Grill	1818 S Osprey Ave	955-7761
Libby's	1917 S Osprey Ave	487-7300
Origin Beer & Pizza	3837 Hillview St	316-9222
Pacific Rim	1859 Hillview St	330-8071
Pazzo Southside	1830 S Osprey Ave	260-8831
Reef Cakes	1812 S Osprey Ave	444-7968
Southside Deli	1825 Hillview St	330-9302
Veronica Fish & Oyster	1830 S Osprey Ave	366-1342

SOUTHGATE		
Restaurant Name	Address	Phone #
Andrea's	2085 Siesta Dr	951-9200
Baker & Wife	2157 Siesta Dr	960-1765
Connors Steakhouse	3501 S Tamiami Trl	260-3232
Fleming's Steakhouse	2001 Siesta Dr	358-9463
Rick's French Bistro	2177 Siesta Dr	957-0533

UNIVERSITY TOWN CENTER (UTC)		
Brio Tuscan Grille	190 Univ Town Ctr Dr	702-9102
Burger & Beer Joint	160 Univ Town Ctr Dr	702-9915
The Capital Grille	180 Univ Town Ctr Dr	256-3647
Cheesecake Factory	130 Univ Town Ctr Dr	256-3760
Kona Grill	150 Univ Town Ctr Dr	256-8005
Rise Pies Pizza	140 Univ Town Ctr Dr	702-9920
Seasons 52	170 Univ Town Ctr Dr	702-9652
Sophies	120 Univ Town Ctr Dr	444-3077

LIVE MUSIC		
Capt. Curt's Oyster Bar	1200 Old Stickney Pt	349-3885
Casey Key Fish House	801 Blackburn Pt Rd	966-1901
Gilligan's Island Bar	5253 Ocean Blvd	349-4759
The Hub Baha Grill	5148 Ocean Blvd	349-6800
JR's Old Packinghouse	987 S Packinghouse	371-9358
Mattison's Forty One	7275 S Tamiami Trl	921-3400

LIVE MUSIC		
Restaurant Name	Address	Phone #
Michael's On East	1212 East Ave	366-0007
Parrot Patio Bar & Grill	3602 Webber St	952-3352
Pop's Sunset Grill	112 Circuit Rd	488-3177
Sharkey's on the Pier	1600 Harbor Dr S	488-1456
Siesta Key Oyster Bar	5238 Ocean Blvd	346-5443
Stottlemeyer's Smokehs	19 East Rd	312-5969
Tamiami Tap	711 S Osprey Ave	500-3182
Walt's Fish Market	4144 S Tamiami Trl	921-4605

CATERING		
The Beach House	200 Gulf Dr N	779-2222
Brick's Smoked Meats	1528 State St	993-1435
Daiquiri Deck Raw Bar	5250 Ocean Blvd	349-8697
Gecko's Grill & Pub	4870 S Tamiami Trl	923-8896
Harry's Continental Kit.	525 St Judes Dr	383-0777
JR's Old Packinghouse	987 S Packinghouse	371-9358
Mattison's Forty One	7275 S Tamiami Trl	921-3400
Michael's On East	1212 East Ave	366-0007
Nancy's Bar-B-Que	301 S Pineapple Ave	366-2271
Sun Garden Café	210 Avenida Madera	346-7170
Village Café	5133 Ocean Blvd	349-2822

EASY ON YOUR WALLET		
Burns Court Cafe	401 S Pineapple Ave	312-6633
Cafe in the Park	2010 Adams Ln	361-3032

EASY ON YOUR WALLET		
Restaurant Name	**Address**	**Phone #**
Casey Key Fish House	801 Blackburn Pt Rd	966-1901
Circo	1435 2nd St	253-0978
El Toro Bravo	2720 Stickney Pt	924-0006
Fresh Start Cafe	630 S Orange Ave	373-1242
Fushipoke	128 N. Orange Ave	330-1795
Gentile Cheesesteaks	7523 S Tamiami Trl	926-0441
Hob Nob Drive-In	1701 Washington Blvd	955-5001
Ichiban Sushi	2724 Stickney Pt Rd	924-1611
Il Panificio	1703 Main St	366-5570
Lovely Square	6559 Gateway Ave	724-2512
Main Bar Sandwich Shp	1944 Main St	955-8733
Mi Tierra Restaurant	1068 N Washington	330-0196
Michelle's Brown Bag	1819 Main St	365-5858
Munchies 420 Café	6639 Superior Ave	929-9893
Nellie's Deli	15 S Beneva Rd	924-2705
New Pass Grill	1505 Ken Thompson	388-3050
Origin Beer & Pizza	3837 Hillview St	316-9222
Origin Beer & Pizza	5070 Clark Rd	217-6533
Pastry Art Bakery	1512 Main St	955-7545
Pho Cali	1578 Main St	955-2683
Piccolo Italian Market	6518 Gateway Ave	923-2202
Rendez-Vous Bakery	5336 Clark Rd	924-1234
Reyna's Taqueria	935 N Beneva Rd	260-8343
Rico's Pizza - Bay Rd	1902 Bay Rd	366-8988
Screaming Goat Taq.	6606 Superior Ave	210-3992
Wicked Cantina	1603 N Tamiami Trl	821-2990

EASY ON YOUR WALLET		
Restaurant Name	**Address**	**Phone #**
Shaner's Pizza	6500 Superior Ave	927-2708
Simon's Coffee House	5900 S Tamiami Trl	926-7151
S Philly Cheesesteaks	1439 Main St	330-8208
Southside Deli	1825 Hillview St	330-9302
Sunnyside Cafe	4900 N Tamiami Trl	359-9500
Tasty Home Cookin'	3854 S Tuttle Ave	921-4969
Tony's Chicago Beef	6569 Superior Ave	922-7979
Yoder's Restaurant	3434 Bahia Vista	955-7771

NEW		
Blase Southern Style	1920 Hillview St.	312-6850
Brine Seafood	2250 Gulf Gate Dr	404-5639
Circo	1435 2nd St	253-0978
Clasico Italian Chophse	1341 Main St	957-0700
1592 Wood Fired Kitch	1592 Main St	365-2234
Flavio's on Main	1766 Main St	960-2305
Fresh Catch Market	7119 S Tamiami Trl	413-7133
Lovely Square	6559 Gateway Ave	724-2512
Mademoiselle Paris	8527 Cooper Creek Bl	355-2323
The Point	135 Bayview Dr	218-6114
Rasoi Indian Kitchen	7119 S Tamiami Trl	921-9200
Reef Cakes	1812 S Osprey Ave	444-7968
Seabar	6540 Superior Ave	923-6605
Smoqehouse	6112 S Tamiami Trl	923-9090
S Philly Cheesesteaks	1439 Main St	330-8208

SPORTS + FOOD + FUN		
Restaurant Name	Address	Phone #
Capt. Curt's Oyster Bar	1200 Old Stickney Pt	349-3885
Daiquiri Deck Raw Bar	5250 Ocean Blvd	349-8697
Gecko's Grill & Pub	6606 S Tamiami Trl	248-2020
Gecko's Grill & Pub	1900 Hillview St	953-2929
Gecko's Grill & Pub	5588 Palmer Crossing	923-6061
Oak & Stone	5405 University Pkwy	225-4590
The Old Salty Dog	5023 Ocean Blvd	349-0158
Parrot Patio Bar & Grill	3602 Webber St	952-3352
Patrick's 1481	1481 Main St	955-1481
Siesta Key Oyster Bar	5238 Ocean Blvd	346-5443

GREAT BURGERS		
Baker & Wife	2157 Siesta Dr	960-1765
Connors Steakhouse	3501 S. Tamiami Trl	260-3232
Gecko's Grill & Pub	4870 S Tamiami Trl	923-8896
Grillsmith's	6240 S Tamiami Trl	259-8383
Gulf Gate Food & Beer	6528 Superior Ave	952-3361
Hob Nob Drive-In	1701 Washington Blvd	955-5001
Indigenous	239 Links Ave	706-4740
Island House Tap & Grl.	5110 Ocean Blvd	312-9205
JR's Old Packinghouse	987 S Packinghouse	371-9358
Knick's Tavern & Grill	1818 S Osprey Ave	955-7761
Made	1990 Main St	953-2900
Mar-Vista Restaurant	760 Broadway St	383-2391
New Pass Grill	1505 Ken Thompson	388-3050
Parrot Patio Bar & Grill	3602 Webber St	952-3352
Patrick's 1481	1481 Main St	955-1481

GREAT BURGERS		
Restaurant Name	Address	Phone #
Shakespeare's Eng Pub	3550 S Osprey Ave	364-5938
Tasty Home Cookin'	3854 S Tuttle Ave	921-4969
Tony's Chicago Beef	6569 Superior Ave	922-7979

NICE WINE LIST		
Andrea's	2085 Siesta Dr	951-9200
Beach Bistro	6600 Gulf Dr N	778-6444
The Beach House	200 Gulf Dr N	779-2222
Bevardi's Salute!	23 N Lemon Ave	365-1020
Bijou Café	1287 First St	366-8111
Café Barbosso	5501 Palmer Crossing	922-7999
Café Gabbiano	5104 Ocean Blvd	349-1423
Café L'Europe	431 St Armands Cir	388-4415
Café Longet	239 Miami Ave W	244-2643
Connors Steakhouse	3501 S Tamiami Trl	260-3232
Dolce Italia	6606 Superior Ave	921-7007
Duval's, Fresh, Local...	1435 Main St	312-4001
Euphemia Haye	5540 Gulf of Mexico Dr	383-3633
Fins At Sharkey's	1600 Harbor Dr S	999-3467
Flavio's Brick Oven	5239 Ocean Blvd	349-0995
Flavio's on Main	1766 Main St	960-2305
Harry's Continental Kit.	525 St Judes Dr	383-0777
Indigenous	239 Links Ave	706-4740
Jack Dusty	1111 Ritz-Carlton Dr	309-2266
Maison Blanche	2605 Gulf of Mexico Dr	383-8088
Mattison's Forty One	7275 S Tamiami Trl	921-3400
Michael's On East	1212 East Ave	366-0007

NICE WINE LIST		
Restaurant Name	Address	Phone #
Miguel's	6631 Midnight Pass	349-4024
Napule Ristorante	7129 S Tamiami Trl	556-9639
Ophelia's on the Bay	9105 Midnight Pass	349-2212
Ortygia	1418 13th Street W	741-8646
Pascone's Ristorante	5239 University Pkwy	210-7268
Pier 22	1200 1st Avenue W	748-8087
Roessler's	2033 Vamo Way	966-5688
Rosebud's Steakhouse	2215 S Tamiami Trl	918-8771
Rosemary & Thyme	511 N Orange Ave	955-7600
Sage	1216 1st St	445-5660
Sardinia	5770 S Tamiami Trl	702-8582

HELP MAKE A DIFFERENCE IN OUR SARASOTA-MANATEE COMMUNITY

Listed below are two local organizations that are striving to assist those in need in our Sarasota area. They could use your help. Please consider a donation to either (or both) during 2021.

ALL FAITHS FOOD BANK
WHAT THEY NEED: Donations of non-perishable, frozen, and perishable food items needed. Monetary donations are also accepted and can be made directly through their website.
MORE INFO: allfaithsfoodbank.org

MAYOR'S FEED THE HUNGRY PROGRAM
WHAT THEY NEED: Donations of food, time, and money are needed. This program hosts a large food drive in the month of November. Check their website for details or to make a monetary donation.
MORE INFO: mayorsfeedthehungry.org

NICE WINE LIST		
Restaurant Name	**Address**	**Phone #**
Selva Grill	1345 Main St	362-4427
Summer House	149 Avenida Messina	206-2675
Waterfront	7660 S Tamiami Trl	921-1916
Veronica Fish & Oyster	1830 S Osprey Ave	366-1342
Viento Kitchen + Bar	4711 Gulf of Mexico Dr	248-1211

A BEAUTIFUL WATER VIEW		
Beach Bistro	6600 Gulf Dr N	778-6444
The Beach House	200 Gulf Dr N	779-2222
Casey Key Fish House	801 Blackburn Pt Rd	966-1901
The Crow's Nest	1968 Tarpon Ctr Dr	484-9551
Drift Kitchen	700 Benjamin Franklin	388-2161
Dry Dock Waterfront	412 Gulf of Mexico Dr	383-0102
Fins At Sharkey's	1600 Harbor Dr S	999-3467
Jack Dusty	1111 Ritz-Carlton Dr	309-2266
Marina Jack's	2 Marina Plaza	365-4243
Mar-Vista Restaurant	760 Broadway St	383-2391
New Pass Grill	1505 Ken Thompson	388-3050
The Old Salty Dog	160 Ken Thompson Pk	388-4311
The Old Salty Dog	1485 S Tamiami Trl	483-1000
O'Leary's Tiki Bar	5 Bayfront Dr	953-7505
Ophelia's on the Bay	9105 Midnight Pass	349-2212
Phillippi Creek Oyster	5363 S Tamiami Trl	925-4444
Pier 22	1200 1st Avenue W	748-8087
Pop's Sunset Grill	112 Circuit Rd	488-3177
The Sandbar	100 Spring Ave	778-0444
Sharkey's on the Pier	1600 Harbor Dr S	488-1456

A BEAUTIFUL WATER VIEW		
Restaurant Name	**Address**	**Phone #**
Snook Haven	500 E Venice Ave	485-7221
Turtle's	8875 Midnight Pass	346-2207
Viento Kitchen + Bar	4711 Gulf of Mexico Dr	248-1211
Waterfront	7660 S Tamiami Trl	921-1916

LATER NIGHT MENU		
Café Epicure	1298 Main St	366-5648
Capt. Curt's Oyster Bar	1200 Old Stickney Pt	349-3885
Circo	1435 2nd St	253-0978
Daiquiri Deck Raw Bar	5250 Ocean Blvd	349-8697
Flavio's Brick Oven	5239 Ocean Blvd	349-0995
Gecko's Grill & Pub	6606 S Tamiami Trl	248-2020
Gecko's Grill & Pub	1900 Hillview St	953-2929
Gilligan's Island Bar	5253 Ocean Blvd	349-4759
Gulf Gate Food & Beer	6528 Superior Ave	952-3361
The Hub Baha Grill	5148 Ocean Blvd	349-6800
Island House Tap & Grl.	5110 Ocean Blvd	312-9205
JR's Old Packinghouse	987 S Packinghouse	371-9358
Mandeville Beer Garden	428 N Lemon Ave	954-8688
Mattison's City Grille	1 N Lemon Ave	330-0440
Monk's Steamer Bar	6690 Superior Ave	927-3388
Munchies 420 Café	6639 Superior Ave	929-9893
Origin Beer & Pizza	3837 Hillview St	316-9222
Origin Beer & Pizza	5070 Clark Rd	217-6533
Parrot Patio Bar & Grill	3602 Webber St	952-3352
Patrick's 1481	1481 Main St	955-1481
Pub 32	8383 S Tamiami Trl	952-3070

LATER NIGHT MENU		
Restaurant Name	Address	Phone #
Sharkey's on the Pier	1600 Harbor Dr S	488-1456
Siesta Key Oyster Bar	5238 Ocean Blvd	346-5443
Walt's Fish Market	4144 S Tamiami Trl	921-4605

SARASOTA FINE & FINER DINING		
Andrea's	2085 Siesta Dr	951-9200
Beach Bistro	6600 Gulf Dr N	778-6444
Bijou Café	1287 First St	366-8111
Café L'Europe	431 St Armands Cir	388-4415
Euphemia Haye	5540 Gulf of Mexico Dr	383-3633
Indigenous	239 Links Ave	706-4740
Jack Dusty	1111 Ritz-Carlton Dr	309-2266
Maison Blanche	2605 Gulf of Mexico Dr	383-8088
Michael's On East	1212 East Ave	366-0007
Ophelia's on the Bay	9105 Midnight Pass	349-2212
Pier 22	1200 1st Avenue W	748-8087
Sage	1216 1st St	445-5660
Summer House	149 Avenida Messina	206-2675

PIZZA PIE!		
Baker & Wife	2157 Siesta Dr	960-1765
Bavaro's Pizza	27 Fletcher Ave	552-9131
Café Barbosso	5501 Palmer Crossing	922-7999
Café Epicure	1298 Main St	366-5648
Caragiulos	69 S Palm Ave	951-0866
Demetrio's Pizzeria	4410 S Tamiami Trl	922-1585

PIZZA PIE!		
Restaurant Name	**Address**	**Phone #**
Flavio's Brick Oven	5239 Ocean Blvd	349-0995
Il Panificio	1703 Main St	366-5570
Main Street Trattoria	8131 Lakewood Main	907-1518
Mattison's City Grille	1 N Lemon Ave	330-0440
Mediterraneo	1970 Main St	365-4122
Napule Ristorante	7129 S Tamiami Trl	556-9639
Oak & Stone	5405 University Pkwy	225-4590
Origin Beer & Pizza	3837 Hillview St	316-9222
Origin Beer & Pizza	5070 Clark Rd	217-6533
Pazzo Southside	1830 S Osprey Ave	260-8831
Rico's Pizza - Bay Rd	1902 Bay Rd	366-8988
Sarasota Brewing Comp	6607 Gateway Ave	925-2337
Shaner's Pizza	6500 Superior Ave	927-2708
Solorzano Bros. Pizza	3604 Webber St	926-4276
Valentino's Pizzeria	4045 Clark Rd	921-9600
Venezia	373 St. Armands Cir	388-1400

UPSCALE CHAIN DINING		
Bonefish Grill	3971 S Tamiami Trl	924-9090
Bravo Coastal Kitchen	3501 S Tamiami Trl	316-0868
Brio Tuscan Grille	190 Univ Town Ctr Dr	702-9102
California Pizza Kitchen	192 N Cattlemen Rd	203-6966
The Capital Grille	180 Univ Town Ctr Dr	256-3647
Carrabba's Italian Grill	1940 Stickney Pt Rd	925-7407
Fleming's Steakhouse	2001 Siesta Dr	358-9463
Kona Grill	150 Univ Town Ctr Dr	256-8005
P.F. Changs	766 S Osprey Ave	296-6002
Seasons 52	170 Univ Town Ctr Dr	702-9652